The Pied Piper

A Play

Peter Terson

A Samuel French Acting Edition

SAMUELFRENCH-LONDON.CO.UK
SAMUELFRENCH.COM

Copyright © 1982 by Peter Terson (book and lyrics) and Jeff Parton (music)
All Rights Reserved

THE PIED PIPER is fully protected under the copyright laws of the British Commonwealth, including Canada, the United States of America, and all other countries of the Copyright Union. All rights, including professional and amateur stage productions, recitation, lecturing, public reading, motion picture, radio broadcasting, television and the rights of translation into foreign languages are strictly reserved.

ISBN 978-0-573-05060-2

www.samuelfrench-london.co.uk

www.samuelfrench.com

FOR AMATEUR PRODUCTION ENQUIRIES

UNITED KINGDOM AND WORLD EXCLUDING NORTH AMERICA

plays@SamuelFrench-London.co.uk

020 7255 4302/01

Each title is subject to availability from Samuel French,
depending upon country of performance.

CAUTION: Professional and amateur producers are hereby warned that THE PIED PIPER is subject to a licensing fee. Publication of this play does not imply availability for performance. Both amateurs and professionals considering a production are strongly advised to apply to the appropriate agent before starting rehearsals, advertising, or booking a theatre. A licensing fee must be paid whether the title is presented for charity or gain and whether or not admission is charged.

The professional rights in this play are controlled by Lemon Unna & Durbridge, Summit House, 170 Finchley Road, London, NW3 6BP.

No one shall make any changes in this title for the purpose of production. No part of this book may be reproduced, stored in a retrieval system, or transmitted in any form, by any means, now known or yet to be invented, including mechanical, electronic, photocopying, recording, videotaping, or otherwise, without the prior written permission of the publisher. No one shall upload this title, or part of this title, to any social media websites.

The right of Peter Terson to be identified as author of this work has been asserted by him in accordance with Section 77 of the Copyright, Designs and Patents Act 1988

THE PIED PIPER

First performed at the Victoria Theatre, Stoke-on-Trent on the 26th November 1980, with the following cast of characters:

Aunty Hamps	Sally Hedges
Polly	Denise Armon
Pally	David Plimmer
Mayor	Tom Bowles
Burgher	Rob Spendlove
Duchess	Diana Kyle
Top Rat	Steven Grenville
Star Rat	{ Tom Bowles { David Bowen
Bar Rat	Rob Spendlove
Pensioner Rat	Ian Reddington
Pied Piper	Ian Reddington
Town Crier	Rob Spendlove
Claude the Cat	David Bowen
Lame Boy	Steven Granville
Chorus, Children etc	

The play directed by Jules Wright
Assisted by Nigel Bryant
Designed by Alwyn James

The action takes place in the town of Hamelin

Songs For
THE PIED PIPER

Music by Jeff Parton

    Fanfare
1. We All Live in Hamelin
2. Rats!
3. The Mayor and Corporation
4. Everybody Wants To Be A Rat
5. Pensioner Rat's Song
6. Pied Piper's Tune
7. We Have a Pest Exterminator
8. Aunty Hamp's Lullaby
9. The Rats Are Busy Tonight
10. We Can't Get Through
11. Pied Piper, Play Your Tune
12. We're Going To Be Rid of the Rats
13. I Want Children
14. The Child Removing Service
15. To A Lovely Joyous Land
16. We're Going To A Magic Land

DIRECTOR'S NOTE

The Pied Piper was commissioned for the Victoria Theatre in Stoke-on-Trent which is a theatre in the round. There are three entrances to the stage in the form of short corridors through the audience. It is a really exciting space in which to do a play, and any hall or large room can be divided up in this way. In our production we used the three stairways into the auditorium as well as the corridors. Of course, *The Pied Piper* can also be done in a proscenium theatre.

We used a company of nine actors several of whom played more than one part. The actors also doubled as musicians so that all of Jeff Parton's music was performed live. We used guitars as well as pipes and percussion. All of the properties and settings, which were minimal, were moved by the actors as part of the action of the play so that each scene flowed into the next and the whole of the theatre was used. Many scenes in the play were tightly choreographed to reinforce the flow of Peter Terson's text.

Lighting and sound played very important parts in creating the atmosphere of this production. I was keen to avoid using conventional stage lighting throughout the production, and to find ways of including the audience in the action of the play. One of the most important elements was a string of very small white fairy lights which completely enclosed the auditorium. Sometimes the stage was lit with just the glimmer of these lights and frequently they were used with the normal stage lighting. The audience was bound with the actors by this ring of white light. The expulsion of the rats from Hamelin was lit by sparklers held by Polly and Pally. Each actor carried three sparklers which were lit one from the other during the action. We also used two echo microphones at opposite ends of the theatre so that the refrain played by the Piper had a haunting, eerie sound. Often another member of the cast played the Piper's tune over a microphone so that the Piper could enter from an unexpected direction.

The play was not set in a specific period. Each character's appearance was created by the designer, Alwyn James, by talking to the author, the actors and me about stories and characters remembered from our childhood.

Finally, the text which is reproduced in this volume is an un-cut version. During the four week rehearsal period we made a number of cuts and this continued throughout the first three performances. Although the script contained here is very long, Peter Terson and I felt that the option to cut should be left to subsequent producers of the play.

Jules Wright

ACT I

On the stage up R *is a table, with three chairs set on top of it. Two red carpet runners are rolled up, one at the entrance down* L, *the other at the entrance down* R

Aunty Hamps enters down L *with a feather duster and dusts the furniture*

Fanfare

Hamps Listen to that fanfare, doesn't it sound grand?
It's not for me, it's for the Mayor and
Corporation close at hand.

Fanfare

They're having a banquet and a feast.
My, I envy them, to say the least.
But there, I'm just here to cook,
Scrub and lay the table.

Fanfare

Come on, children, help Aunty Hamps
As soon as you are able . . .

Polly enters down L *and Pally down* R. *They kick out the red carpets, which form two bright corridors. They carry food, plates, etc., with them*

Polly Coming, Aunty Hampsy, but we're fully laden.
Pally We're her niece and nephew, not beasts of burden . . .
Hamps Never mind complaining—come on at the double,
Or you'll find yourself in severe trouble.
These two are mine. Tablecloth, pronto.

Polly and Pally move the table on the carpet

Polly and Pally,

Hamps puts the chairs round the table

Nephew and niece,
Nice pair of kids
But they give me no peace.
Anyway, I live in Hamelin Town,
By famous Hanover City . . .

Polly and Pally lay the tablecloth and set the table

Polly There she goes again.

Pally	She tells everybody—
Polly `}` **Pally**	That she lives in Hamelin town ... `}`(*Speaking together*)
Hamps	Well I do, and I'm not ashamed of it.
Polly `}` **Pally**	By famous Hanover City. `}`(*Speaking together*)
Hamps	The River Weser deep and wide ...
Polly `}` **Pally**	Washes its wall on the southern side. `}`(*Speaking together*)
Hamps	Don't be cheeky you two. A pleasanter spot you've never spied.

The Lights come up on other members of the cast all over the theatre and they all sing

SONG 1: We All Live In Hamelin

We all live in Hamelin.
By famous Hanover City.
The River Weser deep and wide,
Washes its wall on the southern side.
A pleasanter spot you've never spied.
(*Chorus*)
Hamelin—not Hemmelin
Hamelin to you.
Hamelin, not Homelin.
Not Himmelin, or Hummelin.
Just Hamelin will do.

Polly and Pally run off

Aunty Hamps sets the table from everything about her person: napkins, knives, forks, bowls, all if possible come from herself

Polly and Pally run on and off with various items. The Rats sneak on and hide behind the table

Hamps	Hamelin Town, I love every brick and stone. Another place I wouldn't live. I call this spot my very own ...
Polly	Fish.
Hamps	Look at that for a fish, Caught in our very own River Weser, Fresh from the line.
Polly	Clothes line?
Hamps	Fishing line.
Pally	Chicken.
Hamps	Look at them for chickens! Chuck, chuck— From Hamelin's own farm. Chuck, chuck—I knew that one when it was an egg.

Polly Fruit.

Polly and Pally exit

Hamps Look at that for fruit.
Straight from Hamelin's orchard.
What a spread,
Fit for the Lord Mayor
And his Civic Heads . . .

The Rats, in a spectacular clowning sequence, remove everything from the table

They've gone, GONE—who did it?
Oh, my banquet, oh, my spread.
Who did it to me?
Don't tell me, I know.
It's come into my head.
RATS!
The Ratties—I'll get them.
Come out fighting you rats.

The Rats run across pinching things: passing them, teasing, tormenting, until Aunty Hamps is exhausted, then exit in different directions

Rats . . .

Polly and Pally enter

Polly Did you call?
Pally What's happened, Aunty Hamps?
Hamps Look at the table—look at the disarray,
It's broke my heart, I'm in dismay.
Polly Who was it?
Hamps You should just need one guess.
Pally Give us a clue.
Hamps What can you do?
I'll give you a clue.
They come in swarms, they come in droves,
From out the cellars, from out the groves.
They are a plague, they are a pest,
They give us no peace, give us no rest.
They come in gangs, they come in armies.
They drive you mad, they drive you barmy.
They come by their hundred they come by their thou . . .
Here they come now . . .

The Rats enter from different directions

All Rats . . .
Hamps Get out of it, rats.
Polly It's true, we have a plague.
We've had it weeks, we've had it days.

Pally They passed through one day,
         But they'd come to stay...

Aunty Hamps, Polly and Pally move in slow motion. The Rats move very fast. During the song the Rats remove the table and chairs and roll themselves out in the carpet runners

SONG 2: Rats!

All   Rats! They fight the dogs and tease the cats,
           They rock the babies in their cradles.
           Eat the cheese out of the vats.
Hamps They even lick the cook's own ladles...
All   Rats! they're everywhere.
           In the corner, down the stairs, everywhere.
           Up in the bower, any old hour,
           In the cupboard, like old Mother Hubbard.
           In their fashion, they've taken possession.
Polly They get in my toy box.
Pally Nibble holes in my football socks.
Hamps Take the sequins out of my fancy frocks—
           And furthermore lick all my crocks...
All   Rats!
           They split open the kegs of salted sprats.
           Make nests inside men's Sunday hats.
           And even spoil the women's chats.
           By drowning their speaking,
           With shrieking and squeaking,
           In fifty different sharps and flats.

Fanfare

Hamps Oh, here's the Lord Mayor and his Corporation
           And look at this mess, his banquet,
           Imagine my consternation...

The Mayor, Burgher and Duchess enter down R and move around the stage ceremoniously

Aunty Hamps and Children shudder and shake in a corner. The whole sequence is very formal, like a dance

Mayor   I am the Mayor of Hamelin.

Chord

Duchess I am the Duchess of Hamelin.

Chord

Burgher And I am the Burgher of Hamelin.

Chord

Act I

SONG 3: The Mayor and Corporation

Mayor	We are the Mayor
Duchess ⎫	And Corporation
Burgher ⎭	In a cushy situation.
Mayor	We meet once weekly,
Burgher	Or twice monthly,
Duchess	Or half-yearly,
Mayor	To attend to the business
Burgher ⎫	Of the town:
Duchess ⎭	Or nearly.
All	We sit up in our Town Hall,
	And organize the civic ball,
	Think to give ourselves a treat,
	With best red wine,
	And cuts of meat.
	We rule the town without much haste,
	Make sure there is not any waste.
	To this end we generally taste.
	All the goodies of the town
Burgher ⎫	Personally,
Duchess ⎭	
All	Before they reach the people—
Burgher ⎫	Generally ...
Duchess ⎭	
Mayor	In a word, it isn't a bad life.
	I open a few things with my wife—
Duchess	And I rule with dignity.
	So long as it's good for me.
Burgher	And I deal with forms and dockets,
	So long as it lines my own pockets ...

Chord

Mayor	We are the Mayor
Burgher ⎫	And Corporation
Duchess ⎭	In a cushy situation.
Mayor	We meet once weekly,
Burgher	Or twice monthly,
Duchess	Or half yearly.
Mayor	To attend the business of the town.
Burgher ⎫	Or nearly.
Duchess ⎭	
Mayor	But what's this!
	Where is our banquet woman?
Burgher	Skivvy.
Duchess	Lackey.
All	Where is our banquet?
Hamps	Well your honours, your worships,

	Your highnesses, your reverences—
	Your almighty, your graces—
	It was like this . . .
Mayor	Never mind what it was like. Stop cowering.
Burgher	Quivering.
Duchess	Snivelling.
All	Get us our banquet.
Mayor	Or by my chain of office
	You'll be out of your cottage.
Burgher	Out of a job.
Duchess	Out of town.
Mayor	We can't discuss affairs without sitting down
	To a banquet.
Burgher	And a lot of wine to wash it down.
All	So set us a banquet . . .

The Mayor and Corporation go

Hamps	Well, how do they expect me to find another banquet?
	I can't just conjure one out of mid air.
	That one was all prepared by my own fair hand . . .
	I can't start again.
	I'll be driven from the land.
Pally	Come on Aunty Hamps—we'll help you.
Polly	If we all work together we can get something for them.
Hamps	Boo-hoo, it breaks my heart it really does
	Now I'm threatened with expulsion and eviction.
	And the sack, if I can't find a banquet with some conviction. . . .
	Boo hoo—rats and burghers, they're they bane of my life . . .
Pally	We'll find another banquet *somehow*, Aunty Hamps.
Polly	And as for the rats, we'll pay them back.

Aunty Hamps, Polly and Pally go. Three Rats enter up L, *Top Rat, Star Rat and Bar Rat. Pensioner Rat brings on a deck-chair and sits reading the* Rat Times. *The Musicians enter and sit* C

Top	Hi kids, don't take any notice of them humans—folks
	It's us you're got to watch if you want fun and jokes.
	Introduce yourself, boys.
Star	I'm Star Rat.
	It's stars for me.
	I follow the stars, my way is starred,
	In life I've starred,
	So I wear stars across my bod.
Bar	I'm Bar Rat.
	No bars can hold me,
	And no holds barred with me,
	And from all places I am barred,
	So I wear my bars across my bod.
	Take over, kid.

Act I

Top	I'm Top Rat,
	No top is higher,
	And everything is topped,
	And at everything I'm tops,
	So I wear my top across my bod.
	Now listen, the humans think they own this place,
	Hamelin, but we have it all tied up.
Bar	We've put rats in EVERYWHERE.
Star	The rats we have at our command are—
Top	Great rats, small rats, lean rats, brawny rats,
Star	Brown rats, black rats, grey rats, tawny rats,
Bar	Grave old plodders, gay young friskers.
Top	Fathers, mothers, uncles, cousins,
Star	Cocking tails and pricking whiskers.
Bar	Families by the tens and dozens,
	Brothers, sisters, husbands wives,
	Intend to live here all their lives.
Top	And do you know why these people of Hamelin don't want us?
Bar	He'll tell you why.
Star	Bye and bye, he'll tell you no lie.
Top	I'll tell 'em why.
Bar } Star }	Why?
Top	Why? Because they're jealous.
	You see, everybody wants to be a rat.

SONG 4: Everybody Wants To Be A Rat

Top	Everybody wants to be a rat,
	There's no denying that.
	Who wants to be a boy or girl?
	Going to school to learn nothing at all—
	Running errands at the double—
	Being told off for their trouble—
	It's no fun being a boy or girl.
	Everybody wants to be a rat.
	(*Chorus*)
	Join the gang of gay young friskers,
	Cocking tails and pricking whiskers.
	Everybody wants to be a rat.
Top	Everybody wants to be a rat.
	Man, can you beat that?
	Who wants to be a man, or be a wife,
	Having worries all your life.
	Bring up kids by the score,
	Keeping trouble from the door.
	It's no joy being a man or wife.
	Everybody wants to be a rat.

(*Chorus*)
Join the gang of gay young friskers,
Cocking tails and pricking whiskers.
Everybody wants to be a rat. Yeah!

Pensioner Rat enters

Pensioner You young rats, you young imps,
I want a word with you.
Top Speak on, Grandpa.
Bar If it ain't too much effort.
Pensioner You youngsters are getting the rat colony a bad name.
Bar It's a good name—
Star A great name—
Top A tough name.

The Rats pick up Pensioner in his deck-chair and dance with it

Pensioner That's all very well saying that,
But I've been watching you and come to the conclusion
That you're always in mischief, always in trouble,
You never do things singly when you can do them double.
Top Go get your pension, Grandpa.
Pensioner You cheek all your elders, you never say sir
To help old people you never stir . . .
Bar You're retired, Grandpa—leave over.
Star Life is ours, to take over.
Top You're done, you've had your time,
Take your pension and live in clover.
Come on, gang, if he wants to grumble—
Let's go and cause a rumble.
Pensioner (*to the Audience*)
I don't know what these young rats are coming to, I really don't.

The other Rats and Musicians accompany him

SONG 5: Pensioner Rat's Song

Young rats were never like this in my day,
They'd listen to what their elders had to say.
They were never naughty,
Or haughty.
They were polite and neat,
Cleaned their teeth and wiped their feet.
They were seen, but not heard,
Hung on to every word.
They were very sweet creatures.
They even loved their teachers.
Young rats were never like this in my day.
Young rats weren't like this in my time.

Act I

They believed their elders were right all the time.
They were never rude,
Wouldn't dream of being crude.
They jumped when they were spoken to,
Did what they were told to do.
They were seen, but not heard,
Hung on to every word.
They were tidy and took care.
You could take them everywhere,
They were very sweet creatures
They even loved their teachers.

During the following, the Rats sit Pensioner in his chair and dance off with him down L

All Young rats were never like this in his day.
They didn't get a look in any way.
They were never independent,
Never resplendent,
They were polite and neat.
What a set of creeps,
Young rats were never like us in his day—
Pensioner Pah, they're incorrigible . . .

Bar, Star and Top Rat return

Top Right, gang, let's look for action.
Star What can we do to cause mischief?
Bar A bit of fun, what do you suggest, chief?
Top I'm thinking, can't you hear me thinking?
Some little ruse, some little caper.
Like breaking bottles or tearing paper.
Star We've done all that Top Rat.
Top Wait for it, wait for it.
I tell you we'll have some fun.
We'll get these townsfolk on the run.
I'll lead you where the beans are soaked.
I'll feast you where the bacon's smoked.
Bar I know a dame who's baked new bread.
We'll have some buns, or cakes instead.
Star I know where there's a sweet jar with no lid,
Bar And I know of some little kids,
Who come from school with lollipops,
And ice cream cones and whirly tops.
Top And on the way we'll break some glass.
Leave lots of litter, walk on the grass.
Come on gang, follow me.
For adventure and villainy . . .
But hang on, go no further, pals.
The fun has just begun,

Look at the cute little boy and girl,
We'll offer to join in their fun . . .

Polly and Pally enter down R with a Scarecrow on a barrow

Top	Hi, kids, what's this—he looks a likely pal . . .
Pally	It's a scarecrow, we've made for our Aunty Hamps' vegetable patch.
Star	Look at his nut, it's made of thatch.
Bar	And these clothes he wears to match.
Top	Come on, kids, let's have a game with scarecrow.
Polly	Aunty Hamps wants him to let the plants grow.
Top	Just a little game—we want to get familiar.
Star	Yeah—get to know old scarecrow here.
Polly	We don't want to play with you.
Pally	We know your tricks.
Polly	You nibble all the skipping ropes—and hoops.
Pally	And tie our football nets in loops.
Polly	You frighten all my dolls away.
Pally	Never put our things away.
Polly	And you broke my doll's house up.
Pally	You mixed all my Meccano up.
Top	In a word, you won't play . . .
Star	You won't introduce us to scarecrow?
Polly	In a word, "No."
Top	Well kids, if you won't play voluntarily We'll have scarecrow—he's so solitary. Grab him, rats . . .

The Rats run round with the Scarecrow, keeping Polly and Pally off

Pally	It's our scarecrow, you'll destroy him.
Top	He ain't alive, we can't annoy him.
Polly	You're pulling at his head of straw . . .
Star	He's O.K., he can take some more.
Pally	It's taken ages to complete him . . .
Bar	Now's the time for us to eat him.
Polly / **Pally**	Eat him! } *(Speaking together)*
Rats	Sure, eat him.

There is more scuffling, when suddenly there is the sound of a pipe. Coloured lights flash

Top	Hi, what goes on—why the flashing lights? This ain't a level crossing.

The Rats begin to be paralysed

Bar	I can't move.
Star	And I feel stuck.

Act I

Polly What wonderful music, it's like a dream.
Pally I don't understand it, what can it mean?

The Pied Piper appears suddenly at the top of the stairs

Top Well I'll be blowed...
Bar I can move again, it must have been cramp.
Top Who's this jerk?
Star Who is this colourful tramp?
Polly Excuse me, sir—but *who are you*?
Piper (*walking on to the stage*)
 You can say I am a travelling man,
 I come and go, where I can.
 Around my neck is my only possession.
 My pipe—with which I carry out my profession.
Pally You *live* by your pipe?
Piper I play for my supper, I play for my bed,
 I play for my dinner, I play for my bread,
 I play in the spring, when the small birds hatch,
 I play in the summer, under the thatch,
 I play in the autumn as the apples get riper,
 I play in the winter, and people call me, the Pied Piper.
Pally⎫
Polly⎭ The Pied Piper! } (*Speaking together*)
Top The Pied Piper.
 Have you seen anything so ridiculous,
 Anything so phoney?
 He is so much flesh and bone,
 I would call him Boney.
Piper The Pied Piper, if you please.
Pally⎫
Polly⎭ Yes, the Pied Piper, if you please. } (*Speaking together*)
Bar The Pied Piper.
 With a queer long coat from heel to head,
 Half of yellow and half of red,
 And he himself, so tall and thin,
 With sharp blue eyes each like a pin,
 He is so much bone and skin,
 I would call him Skinny.
Piper The Pied Piper, if you please.
Pally⎫
Polly⎭ Yes, the Pied Piper, if you please. } (*Speaking together*)
Star The Pied Piper!
 With light loose hair, and swarthy skin,
 No tuft on cheek, nor beard on chin.
 And lips where smiles go out and in,
 There is no guessing his kith or kin,
 I would call him Grinny.
Piper The Pied Piper, if you please.

Polly **Pally** {	The Pied Piper, if you please. } (*Speaking together*)
Piper	And tell me, I heard your cries, Tell me where the trouble lies.
Polly	They've taken our scarecrow we made to keep the birds away,
Pally	And they'll destroy him if they go on this way.
Piper	If they want the scarecrow let them keep him, You could do worse. I'll blow them a tune to make their privilege a curse.
Top	All right, rats, let's play on.
Piper	If you insist on causing strife— Perhaps the scarecrow can have some life.

The Piper plays. The Scarecrow comes to life

Rats   With a queer long coat, from heel to head,
Half of yellow and half of red,
And he himself so tall and gawky,
And his pipe so shrill and squawky...

The Scarecrow dances with the Rats and they notice him

Top   Eek—he's come to life.
Bar   Run, boys, for your life.

The Scarecrow generally bats them around

Piper   Now, I think they've had enough.
I'll return the scarecrow to old straw and stuff.

The Scarecrow goes back into the barrow

Pally   But he came to life—he breathed, he walked, he ran...
Piper   Now he'll do his job, take him to the garden as fast as you can.

The Pied Piper goes down R

Polly   Well thank you Pied Pi... He's gone.
Pally   That was strange. Come, let's get on.

Polly and Pally go with Scarecrow up C

Top (*recovering*)
    Now I've got my mad up.
    He plays his pipe all right.
    To give us a nasty fright.
    We'll play the next tune for his cheek.
    Call up the rat bugler, let him squeak,
    And to the colony I'll speak.
    I'll call on my rat lads everywhere.
    We'll call...

Rats   Great rats, small rats, lean rats, brawny rats,
Brown rats, black rats, grey rats, tawny rats,
Grave old plodders, gay young friskers,
All our brothers, all our cousins,

Act I

	Tearaway rats by the dozens.
Top	Call every likely rat to start,
	We're going to pull this town apart.
Star	What are we going to do, Top Rat?
Top	We're going to take the lid off custard tarts,
	We're going to pull the pantries all apart.
	We'll go to war ...
Bar	War, what shall we use for weapons?
Top	Our weapons is our teeth. Prepare to gnaw.
	We'll take over Hamelin from the people.
	From the Town hall to the church steeple.
	We'll nibble at their buildings till they crumble,
	We'll chew at roots till trees tumble,
	We'll bite through all the water pipes,
	Eat all the meats and all the tripes,
	We'll nibble through the warehouse ropes,
	So the merchants give up hope,
	And we'll take over Hamelin from the people.
Star	A full-scale war—wow, what a whizz.
Bar	I'll live on chocolate bars and lemon fizz.
Top	Right, lads, let all rats pillage,
	Let the kingdom never be quiet,
	Start to squeak, break into a riot ...

The Rats exit up R *with squeaks and uproar. Aunty Hamps, Polly and Pally enter with a table laden with dishes and food, which they proceed to lay out*

Hamps	Here we go again, second time lucky,
	To prepare a banquet for the Mayor,
	And his Corporation,
	We must be daft or plucky.
	Come on Polly and Pally, I can't do it on my own,
	Lay their table until it groans.
Pally	You work like a slave for this Corporation.
Polly	And not a word of thanks or consolation.
Hamps	Oh I know it, they take me for an absolute nelly,
	They're only happy when I'm filling their—tummies.

The Rats enter down R, L *and* C

	It's gone—my ham—I saw it vanish in a flash ...
Pally	Rats, after them ...
Hamps	Quick, dash.
	Get it back, it's my last chance ...

Fanfare. They chase round the Rats, who throw the ham backwards and forwards to each other

Eventually the Rats go off in triumph. The Mayor, Duchess and Burgher enter down R

The following scene is choreographed

All	We are the Mayor and Corporation,
	In a cushy situation.
	We meet once weekly,
	Or twice monthly,
	Or half-yearly,
	To attend to the business
	Of the town.
	Or nearly . . .
Mayor	And now for our banquet . . .
Duchess	But where IS our banquet?
Burgher	Woman—explain yourself. Our banquet . . .
All	We can't take a decision without a banquet.
	We can't rule the town without it:
	Or make the laws, or raise the rents and rates,
	Or attend the long debates,
	Until we've had our banquet.
Hamps	I'm sorry Mr Mayor and Corporation,
	But this time you'll have to do without a banquet.
Mayor	Impossible.
Burgher	Out of the question.
Duchess	Unthinkable.
Mayor	You're fired.
Pally	Fired—but she worked so hard . . .
Hamps	And I'm just a poor woman,
	I work each night and day.
	I work my fingers to the bone,
	For very little pay.
	Look at my knees, red raw,
	And my back, bent double.
	I can't do more.
	Give me a chance, there is an explanation.
Polly	She can explain the situation.
Mayor	No excuse—you are fired.
	There can be no excuse.
Hamps (*on her dignity*)	
	Oh, no excuse indeed, I've had enough,
	Of being pushed round and treated rough.
	I'll give you in one word the explanation,
	Mr Mayor, and your bleeding Corporation.
All	One word.
Hamps	One word—RATS.
	Never mind your banqueting,
	Your wining and your dining,
	Your feasting and your junketing,
	Do your duty and face the facts,
	This town is plagued with rats.

Act I

Mayor	Rats? (*He jumps up on a table*)
Hamps	Yes, rats, they're running riot.
Duchess	Rats? Indeed. (*She jumps up on the table*)
Hamps	Yes, you cannot keep them quiet.
Burgher	Rats? Really? (*He jumps up on the table*)
Hamps	Yes, just listen, really try it.
	Can't you hear them above your speaking?
Hamps ⎫	Scratching and nibbling and squealing and squeaking,
Pally ⎬	Running, and jumping, biting and rushing.
Polly ⎭	Don't you hear them above your debate?
	Hurry, hurry, before it's too late.
Polly	Don't you realize? All the people to the town hall in a body,
	Have come flocking.
Pally	"Tis clear," cry they, "our Mayor's a Noddy."
Mayor	Me? A Noddy?
Hamps	And as for our Corporation, shocking.
	To think we buy gowns lined with ermine,
	For dolts who won't, or can't determine,
	What's best to rid us of our vermin.
Polly ⎫	Rouse up, sirs, give your brains a racking. ⎫ (*Speaking*
Pally ⎭	To find the remedy we're lacking. ⎭ *together*)
Hamps	Or sure as fate we'll send you packing.
	Come on, children, let's lock all the cupboards—
	Bolt up the doors, to stop the rats,
	We'll nail down the floors . . .

Aunty Hamps, Pally and Polly go down R

Mayor	Well, we MUST do something.
Burgher	We HAVE to do something.
Duchess	I find rats no problem, they'd don't get into *my* palace.
Burgher	And they don't eat at *my* profits.
Mayor	But as the elected representatives of the poor,
	We have to make a show.
	Why don't we elect a town rat exterminator?
	We'll ask him how he did it later.
	We'll make a show of effort, don't you know.
Burgher	As the elected councillors of the populace,
	We dare not fall into disgrace.
	Why don't we buy some extras snares and traps
	So we don't take any raps?
	And our efforts will have saved us face.
Duchess	As a member of the aristocratic class,
	It's come to a very pretty pass.
	Why don't we give the common folk bait and poison
	And let them deal with it in person.
	Let the effort be taken by the mass . . .

Aunty Hamps enters with Polly and Pally down R

During the following Aunty Hamps chases them. She runs up and over the table repeatedly as if it did not exist

Hamps	Well, have you found the answer?
	Have you found a way to rid the town of rats?
Mayor	Don't hurry us—we thought we'd hold a meeting—
Burgher	To discuss it—
Duchess	Over a banquet.
Hamps	This won't do, this won't do.
Polly }	This won't do, this won't do.
Pally	
Hamps	To think we buy gowns lined with ermine,
	For dolts who won't, or can't determine.
Polly }	What's best to rid us off our vermin.
Pally	
All	This won't do, this won't do.
	No it won't, this won't do.
Mayor	It's easy to bid one rack one's brain.
	I've thought and thought, but all in vain.
Duchess	There is no answer that is plain.
Burgher	The problem drives us quite insane.
Hamps	This won't do—
Pally	This won't do—
Polly	No, it won't—
All	This won't do.
Hamps	Rouse up, sirs, give your brains a racking,
	Or sure as fate we'll send you packing.
Mayor }	
Duchess }	Packing?
Burgher }	
Hamps	If you insist on doing nought,
	The townsfolk will vote you out.
Mayor }	
Duchess }	Vote us out?
Burgher }	
Hamps }	
Polly }	OUT.
Pally }	
Hamps	Get rid of the rats.
Mayor	But we can't do it.
Burgher	We don't know how.
Duchess	We can't attempt it.
Hamps	Then find somebody who can.
Mayor	We haven't got anybody.
Hamps	Then ADVERTISE!
	For truly this town has had enough.
	Of you drinking wine and sniffing snuff,
	You sit on your backsides making decrees,

Act I

	While we suffer from these rats with fleas.
	I'm warning you, Mayor, and Corporation,
	Do something, while you have the townsfolk's co-operation.
	This won't do, this won't do . . .
Hamps	To think we voted into power,
Pally	These geese who do nothing by the hour.
Polly	This won't do. This won't do.
	No it won't. This won't do.
Mayor	Oh, what can we do?
Duchess	Advertise man, you heard, the woman ADVERTISE!
Mayor	Right, call out the Town Crier,
	To find a man we can pay or hire—
	To anyone who can rid us of our rats,
	We'll give a reward, let's try at—
	A hundred gilders.
Burgher	A hundred—
	Make it five hundred.
Duchess	Five hundred, make it a thousand.
Polly Pally	A thousand, make it ten thousand.
Mayor	Ten thousand, but there'll be nothing left in the coffers,
	If we go on making these gigantic offers.
Hamps	But if the rats eat us out of house and home
	Out in the wilderness we'll be forced to roam.
	I say—to anyone—near or far,
	Great or small,
	Short or tall,
	Black or white—
	Who can rid us of this plague of rats—
	Fifty thousand gilders would be quite right.
All	Fifty thousand gilders.
Hamps	That's what I say—and cheap at the price.
	For anyone who can rid us of the rats,
	I wouldn't think twice.

Hamps sits triumphantly on the table

Mayor	Fifty thousand then it is.
	Call the Town Crier,
	Tell him put a new clapper in his bell.
	Raise his voice the news to tell,
	Fifty thousand gilders reward to any genius
	To rid us of the rats who come between us
	And the prosperity and happiness of our town—
	Fifty thousand, not a penny less—even if I pawn my gown.

Polly and Pally carry Aunty Hamps off on the table

	We're going to be rid of the rats.
Polly Pally	The town will be happy again. No need to lock up your sweets, Or hide your treats. We're going to be rid of the rats ...
Mayor Duchess Burgher	We're going to be rid of the rats. We'll be in office again. We'll start now before it's too late, Then have a banquet to celebrate, We're going to be rid of the rats ...

The Mayor and the Burgher exit down R

The Duchess starts up the stairs C

Top Rat enters down the stairs L

Top	Say, Duchess, will you excuse me a minute?
Duchess	Who are you? Are you a rat?
Top	Now Duchess, is that any way to speak to a gentleman? Am I a rat? I am a King.
Duchess	A king?
Top	Among my own sort. Now I have a proposition to put to you On behalf of the furry kingdom.
Duchess	The furry kingdom?
Top	Yeah, my folks. You might like to call them rats We refer to ourselves as the FURRY KINGDOM.
Duchess	What's this proposition?
Top	Just this, Duchess— You leave us alone, and we leave you alone.
Duchess	But the Mayor is already advertising for a Rat Exterminator.
Top	That's the Mayor—I'll deal with him later. But now We want *you* on our side.
Duchess	On your side?
Top	Look at it this way, Duchess— The rats of this world need a friend We come to *you* for this end. If you help us gain the town complete, We'll leave you in your palace replete, With everything you need We can provide, Everything that we gain, With you divide. Now, for a start, Duchess, Is there anything you want? Anything you savour? Any work, any favour?
Duchess	Now you mention it, I need my vast lawns trimmed.
Top	I'll put five thousand nibblers on it in the morning.
Duchess	And I'd like my cellars with wine filled.

Act I

Top	Burgundy, sherry, Madeira, or hock. Name it, we'll bring the lot.
Duchess	And my palace needs a coat of paint.
Top	I'll get some of my best bristlers on the job, They'll work without restraint. And give it a coat at the whisk of a tail.
Duchess	One thing more ...
Top	Name it.
Duchess	My price, for joining in your scheme. I've always had a little dream ...
Top	Reveal it.
Duchess	I'd like two young human slaves. Children who I could train. To do my bidding, wait on me hand and foot. Lay my table, iron my linen, light my fires. And cook. At the end of the day, With lock and key, I'd fasten them in my dungeon. Quite privately.
Top	Er, Duchess, any child slaves in particular?
Duchess	Yes, I've noticed them. They have an Aunt with whom they dwell, Here they come, they would do quite well.
Top	Come midnight, we'll have them for you. ....

Top Rat exits down R

Polly and Pally enter down L, *Polly on a wooden scooter*

Polly	Brother, the Duchess, why is she looking at us?
Pally	She has a right to look ...
Polly	But so strangely, and whispering with Top Rat.
Pally	I must say I don't like that.
Duchess	Good morning, children, you look so happy every day, Enjoy your freedom while you may. Carry on.

The Duchess goes up the stairs C

Polly	I don't like it, she's quite frightening.
Pally	Don't worry, she can't harm us. Only the rats we have to fear. But here comes the Town Crier to Make his announcement, Let's draw near.

The Town Crier enters with his hand-bell. He takes off his top hat, which is reinforced with metal, and stands on it

Crier	Oyez, oyez, now listen here.

The whole Company enter

        The Mayor and Corporation have issued a decree

	For anyone to hear, and anyone to see.
	That from this date and present time
	The person who can by wit or guile,
	Rid this town of its plague of pestering rats
	Will be rewarded, JUST LIKE THAT.
	Fifty thousand gilders—
All	Fifty thousand gilders—
Crier	is on offer
	Who will take up the challenge?
	For who succeeds, we will fill his coffer.
All	Who can we find to end the plague we suffer?
	To rid the nuisance there's nothing tougher.
	RATS...

All sing and dance the following sequence, which is choreographed

SONG 2 (reprise): Rats!

	They fight the dogs and tease the cats,
	They rock the babies in their cradles,
	They eat the cheeses out of the vats,
	They lick the soup from the cooks' own ladles.
Crier	Fifty thousand gilders—
All	Fifty thousand gilders—
Crier	to anyone who can
	Rid the town of rats...
All	They split open the kegs of salted sprats
	Make nests inside men's Sunday hats,
	And even spoil the women's chats
	By drowning their speaking,
	With shrieking and squeaking,
	In fifty different sharps and flats.
Crier	Fifty thousand gilders—
All	Fifty thousand gilders—
Crier	to anyone who can
	Rid this town of rats.

Claude the Cat enters down C

Claude	What's this? A contract?
Crier	Yes, you must be a stranger here?
Claude	I'm just passing through, not to linger,
	If you could spare me a penny for a fish or fish finger.
Crier	A penny! The Mayor and Corporation are
	Offering FIFTY THOUSAND gilders to anyone—
	Man, woman, beast, or cat—to anyone who
	Can rid us of the very last rat.
Claude	Now isn't that a coincidence?
	Can you credit such a thing?
	Can you guess what my trade is?

Act I

Polly Your trade? Are you a plumber?
Claude No, my trade has nothing to do with sinks,
Have another thinks.
Pally A grocer?
Claude No, I don't work behind a counter,
But as this is your first encounter
With a man of my profession I'll put you in the picture.
I am first, and foremost, a fully trained,
Highly skilled—rat-catcher.
All A rat-catcher.
Claude The very same.
That's the name of my game.
Crier But can you rid us of a plague?
Claude A plague? The more they come,
The more I like it.
I'm Claude the Cat,
The master of any rat.
When they see me they cringe in terror.
When I go to work there is no error.
Rats, I'll rid this town in days.
Rats, they'll get to know my ways.

Top Rat appears

Top Who is this guy shouting off his mouth?
Claude I'm Claude, the pest exterminator,
I get them all, sooner or later.
When they see me they pack their bags and cases,
Hide their heads and cover up their faces.
Rats, there will be none left in Hamelin Town,
Rats, they know of my renown.
EEEK—what was that . . .
Polly Just a rat.
Claude A rat?
Pally One of the millions.
Claude Great, shucks, I can't wait to start.

SONG 7: We Have a Pest Exterminator

All We have a pest exterminator.
The rats will know, sooner or later,
That in Hamelin we won't tolerate,
Rats who come and live in state,
Rats who under floorboards live,
Rats who take but never give.
Rats who eat right through a tin,
Rats who create an awful din,
Rats who squeal and rats who squeak,
Rats who'll know within a week,
That their reign is over.

Claude	Well, do you vote me in?
All	Do we vote him in?
Crier	Ladies and gentlemen, townsfolk of Hamelin,
	Silence while we take a vote,
	For Claude the Cat of famous note—
	As our official exterminator of rats.

All cheer. There is the sound of a flute from the stairs C

Polly	Just a minute—there may be another candidate.
Claude	Another candidate. Are you kidding?
	I am renowned for my rat extermination,
	Who else is there with my reputation?

The Pied Piper appears on the stairs C

Piper	There is ME.
All	Who is this?
Polly / **Pally**	He's the Pied Piper.
Hamps	You've met him?
	Why didn't you tell your Aunty?
	He's lovely. Hello, Pied.
	I'm their Aunty Hamps.
Crier	Do you mean to tell us that you wish to apply for the job of ridding us of the rats?
Piper	I do.
Crier	Then we must accept the nomination.
Claude	Nonsense, what can he do?
	Look at me, I have claws, I have teeth,
	I can jump, I can pounce,
	Look at him, weighing half an ounce—
	With a queer long coat from heel to head,
	Half of yellow and half of red,
	And he himself so tall and gawky,
	And his pipe so shrill and squawky.
	He isn't equipped to deal with your problem.
	Leave them to me, I'll soon nobble 'em.
Crier	This is a decision for the Mayor and Corporation,
	The two candidates will meet in the morning,
	At the Town Hall and present their credentials.
	It will be a vote between Claude the Cat
	And—er—what name shall I announce?
Polly / **Pally**	The Pied Piper (*Speaking together*)
Crier	Quite so, the Pied Piper—so everyone,
	All return to your homes even though
	Rat infested.
	Tomorrow our official exterminator will be invested.

The Town Crier and Townspeople exit

Act I

Claude	It's a pushover.
Top	Let me see you home, buddy.
Claude	Eeek, a rat ...

Claude the Cat dashes off up C

Hamps	Have you anywhere to stay, Pied Piper?
Piper	I'll find a place.
	I play my pipe for my butter and my bread,
	And for a place to rest my head.
Polly	Let him stay with us, Aunty Hamps.
Hamps	Well, shall I? Shall I not?
	I don't know what the neighbours will think.
	I don't have visitors a lot.
Polly	Please, Aunty Hamps, please.
Hamps	He certainly looks a quiet fellow,
	With his coat half of red and half of yellow
	I could give him his supper and a couch,
	He doesn't look any sort of slouch.
	But you promise you'll play your pipe on request?
	I have a little need of piping.
Piper	I'll do my best.

They all go. The Duchess enters with Top Rat down the stairs L

Top	There go the children you require, Duchess.
Duchess	To have two slaves is my heart's desire.
	Can you get them?
Top	Am I a liar?
	It's all organized.
	I have alerted the whole rat kingdom,
	They have dug tunnels and catacombs,
	From your dungeon, to the children's room.
	As soon as I give the whistle for the plan to start,
	They'll bring to the window a horse and cart
	And hanging together tip to tail.
	They'll make a rope of rat-like style,
	And we'll whisk the children off to your palace,
	Many a mile, before the alarm is raised.
	Come on, gang, let all rats be praised.

The Duchess and Top Rat go down R. Polly and Pally enter down C with a bed. Pally has his guitar

Polly and Pally put the bed up L and sit on it. Moonlight shines through the window on to the floor. Pally has his guitar and strums

Aunty Hamps enters with a lantern

Hamps	I wish I could get those children to sleep.
	Honestly, they're so excited they'll never settle.
	Come on, children, time for bye-byes,

	Shut eye, kip, head down.
	Aunty insists, Aunty demands,
	Aunty orders it—SLEEP.
Polly	But we can't sleep, Aunty.
Pally	It's been such an exciting day, and it's the election tomorrow.
Hamps	Lie down, and I'll tell you a story.
Polly	We know your stories.
Pally	They're always the same—about the prince, falling in love— with you.
Hamps	What's wrong with that?
Polly	It's so *unlikely*.
Hamps	I could have married a prince, or a king, or a duke, years ago.
Pally	If they'd asked.
Hamps	If I hadn't had you two to look after.
	Now lie down and I'll sing you a lullaby.
Pally } Polly }	A lullaby, not that, with your voice.
Hamps	Nothing wrong with my voice.
	It would charm a chicken from a tree,
	Or a goose from his hoose.
	Or a turkey from Alberquerquay,
	Enough, prepare to shut eye.
	Aunty Hamps is about to sing her lullaby.

Aunty Hamps sings in an appalling voice

SONG 8: Aunty Hamps' Lullaby

	The cloak of night has stolen over the city,
	The lamplighters gone to bed.
	There's none so handsome, there's none so pretty,
	As on the pillow where I lay my head . . .
Chorus	Lay my head, lay my head.
	On the pillow where I lay my head.

A rope ladder is let in from the roof

Polly	Listen, Aunty,
Hamps	How can I listen when I'm *singing*?

Another rope ladder is let in

Pally	Rest your voice, then, and listen.
Polly	The rats are so active.
Pally	They're up to something.
Polly	Hustling and bustling.
Pally	Lifting latches,
	Opening catches.
Polly	Sneaking downstairs,
	Whispering in lairs.

Act I

Pally	Laying up schemes,
	Stopping our dreams.
Polly	Scraping and scratching,
	Something they're hatching.

A trapeze is let in from the roof

Pally⎫	The rats are busy tonight.
Polly⎭	It's no use Aunty, we'll never get to sleep.
Hamps	Never?
Pally⎫	
Polly⎭	No, never
Hamps	Without a doubt?
Pally⎫	Sleep is out—
Polly⎭	For the rats are busy tonight.

SONG 9: The Rats Are Busy Tonight

All	The rats are busy tonight.
	Picking locks,
	Taking stocks.
	Opening windows,
	Frightening widows.
	Planning something.
	Can't be nothing.
	The rats are busy tonight.

A rope is let in

Hamps	They *do* sound suspiciously active,
	What can they be doing?

The remaining ropes are let in

> *Top Rat, Star Rat and Top Rat enter down* L. *They swing around from rope to rope, to the ladder above the bed, etc.*

The ropes, etc. are pulled after the last Rat has moved on

Top	O.K. rats, you're my chosen band.
	The children's room is close at hand.
	We've got to get up there
	and snatch them quick.
	This trapeze should do the trick.
Star	Trapeze? Isn't a trapeze
	Only worked with ease
	By acrobats?
Top	Sure, acrobats or active rats.
	Can you do it, or can you not?

	There's plenty more where you came from, To stop the rot.
Bar	Sure, we can do it chief, Takes a bit of handling, that's all.
Top	Well, handle it. I want you up there like a thief.

They try the trapeze, but are hopeless

Top	Not good at all. I'll make it easy so you won't fall. Send down the rope ladder, Any size, it doesn't matter.

The rope ladder comes down

Star	That's better, a rope ladder with rungs.
Bar	Now the fun has just begun.
Top	Then up there—follow me.
Bar	This is as easy as can be.
Top	Sure, sure. Hi, what's the matter with you?
Star	Boss, boss, I feel a bit dizzy, I haven't got no head for heights. I'm in a tizzy.

They juxtaposition

Bar	Hi boss, I think you should supervise him going down. You got a stronger tail than me to help him on.
Top	Okay. Every man at his station stay, We'll soon have him under way.

They climb round, get in a tangle and fall

Pensioner Rat enters down L with his umbrella as the last Rat swings off

Pensioner	You young rats, what are you doing?
Top	Keep out of this, Grandad.
Bar	Keep your nose clean.
Top	This is top secret.
Star	Yeah, we're going to kidnap the kids.
Bar	From their very own bedroom.
Top (*banging their heads together*)	
	Top secret, can I not give you any trust? I'll bang your heads like a pair of nuts.
Pensioner	Kidnap children?
Top	Keep out of this, Grandpa.
Pensioner	Such folly I'll never understand. Don't you know the laws of Ratland? Never meddle in human affairs. A man's home is his castle, Yours is your lairs.
Top	Now listen, Grandpa—your day is over. We have a treaty with the Duchess, That will keep us in clover.

Act I

Bar For Hamelin we mean to take over.
Pensioner But you mustn't kidnap human boys and girls. (*He reaches out with his umbrella*)

The umbrella is caught on the trapeze and hauled out

Top Try stopping us, Grandpa.
Come on lads, around he twirls.
Bar You'll never get away with it.

Pensioner Rat exits down L

Back to the Children and Aunty Hamps. During the song the Rats swing on their journey and finish on the rope ladder above the bed

SONG 9 (reprise): The Rats Are Busy Tonight

Pally
Polly } The rats are so busy tonight.
Polly They are preparing,
To be more daring.
Pally Leaving their lairs,
Running in pairs.
Polly Making trouble.
At the double.
Pally Up to something.
Can't be nothing.
Pally
Polly } The rats are busy tonight.
Hamps Now, children, are you still not asleep?
Polly It's no use Aunty, listen to the noise.
Pally I'll never sleep, I wish it would stop.
Hamps If you wish hard enough, it might stop.
Pally
Polly } We both wish the rat noise would stop.

Suddenly there is the sound of a pipe. The rat noise stops and the Rats freeze

Polly The rat noise *has* stopped.
Pally Definitely dropped.

The Pied Piper enters

Pally Piper, it's you.
Polly And it was *you* who silenced the rats.
Hamps I wish you and your pipe could get these two to sleep.
Polly Impossible.
Pally More than improbable.
Polly He'd never get us to close our eyes.
Hamps I wish he would, off to bye-byes.

The Pied Piper smiles and pipes and they go slowly off to sleep

Polly	We told you—
Pally	You couldn't—
Polly	Get us to—
Pally } **Polly** }	Sleep.
Hamps	Well, if you think they're asleep, quite tight,
	I think I'll turn in myself for the night.
	Good night, Piper—(*yawn*)—dear Piper Pied—
	He doesn't answer, he must be tongue-tied . . .

She is lulled to sleep

Piper	Before I take a rest myself, my beauties,
	I'll have a little tour of duty,
	To put my mind at ease.
	The rats have been so active,
	In a way that doesn't please.

He goes into the shadows and exits down L

The Rats climb down the ladder

The Duchess enters down R

Top	Now, Duchess, we've promised you two children to be your slaves.
Bar	We'll do it quick, your time to save.
Duchess	These are the children I want for my scheme,
	They'll be in my dungeon when they come
	Out from their dream . . .
Top	You better have a good look, Duchess, a glance,
	We don't want to snatch the wrong pair by mischance.
Duchess	These are the ones, I've noticed them many times before.
	Take them, I want them on my dungeon floor.
Top	You're quite emphatic?
Bar	This could be traumatic.
Top	Go closer, check their identity.
Star	We want to complete this job in its entirety.

The Duchess goes closer—reaches out to touch them, but the pipe plays

Duchess	That's funny, I cannot get through to them.
	It's as if they're surrounded by a curtain,
	Or a barrier of invisible power, I'm not certain.
Top	Come off it, Duchess—invisible curtains!
	Nonsense, there's nothing there.
	Show her, Bar, so she'll be certain.
Bar	Sure boss. I don't need alertin'.

Bar Rat makes a run at it, but bounces off

Bar	That's funny, I bounced off as if it was rubber,
	Or else an invisible wall of whale blubber.

Act I

Top Stand back, will you, I'll do it myself.
I have led you lot and never bumped yet.
See these whiskers, they sniff out every
Barrier, nothing stops me . . .
Bar It's true, nothing stops Top Rat.
He's been to the top of St Paul's dome,
Star And the High Vatican in Rome.
Bar He was in the first rat team to climb Everest.
Star And the Matterhorn north face was a severe test.
Bar He was in a Rat Circus troupe.
Star And walked the high wire and looped the loop.
Top In a word, Duchess, there ain't a barrier been made
That can stop me.

He goes at it, but bumps back

That's queer, I can't get through.
Bar And I can't get through.

The Rats and Duchess sing and dance round the bed

SONG 10: We Can't Get Through

Rats
Duchess
We can't get through, we can't get through.
Not over it, or under it.
Not by it, or through it,
Not round it, or bypass it.
Isn't it frustrating,
Ain't it aggravating,
We can't get through.

We can't get through, we can't get through
Not even if we push it,
Or almighty rush it.
It's just too much.
Isn't it frustrating,
Ain't it aggravating,
We can't get through.
Hamps Rats! Sound the alarm!
Top Quick, rats, scarper . . .

She brings out a gong

Hamps Rats, rats, rats in the night.
Rats up to no good.
Rats are here all right!

The Rats go

Hamps Duchess, what are *you* doing here?
Duchess Oh, I was passing in my carriage,
When I saw the rats entering your house:

	So I followed them in,
	To prevent them doing mischief...
Hamps	Well, isn't that nice? Thank you, Duchess.
	She's real quality. Thank you, my lady.
Duchess	That's all right, carry on.

The Duchess goes off down R

Hamps   Well now is the day for the great selection,
Between the Pied Piper and Claude the Cat,
Some election!
I hope it's the Piper, I do
Not only because of the rats,
But because of him, I'll tell you.
Even though he is a strange feller.
With his queer long coat, from heel to head
Half of yellow and half of red,
And he himself so tall and thin,
With sharp blue eyes, each like a pin,
And light loose hair, that swarthy skin,
Not tuft on cheek, nor beard on chin,
But lips where smiles go out and in.
There is no guessing his kith and kin.
I cannot quite enough admire.
That sweet man and his quaint attire.
His tune sets my little soul on fire.

She sings

SONG 11: Pied Piper Play Your Tune

Pied Piper, play your tune,
Play it sweet and play it soon.
Soft as the gentle breeze,
Or the whisper of the trees.
Listen to the lovely melody.
It's played for you, it's played for me.

She shakes the children

Come on, wake up, children.
Wake up.
I can't wake them up you know, they sleep like logs,
Once they go off they're like lazy dogs.

Polly   Is it time to get up?
Hamps   Come on you lazy pair.
Time for us to go to the Town Square.
To see the choice of the rat catcher.
Will it be the Pied Piper?
Or Claude the Scratcher?
Pally   The election—let's hurry and support the Pied Piper.

Act I

Hamps Time to get breakfast, and time to wash behind your ears.
There's time to get there, have no fears.

They all exit, Polly and Pally carrying off the bed up C. Claude the Cat enters down L

Claude This is the day of the big choice.
Am I nervous? Does it tell in my voice?
On this decision rests my whole career.
If I fail I won't be long here.
I'll be on the road again, begging and borrowing,
A life of hunger always following.
Still let's look on the bright side,
I'll give an impression of calm on the outside.

Top Rat comes in and tweeks Claude

Claude Eeek—a rat ...
Top Stay where you are, Buster!
So, you're planning to exterminate us.
Claude Just if it's in the contract ...
Top Sure, go ahead—we like a worthy opponent.
Like yourself.
Better you than that Pied Piper.
Claude Oh, thanks, Rat ...
Top Yeah, a cat is a cat, I can understand that.
He has claws, he has paws I can deal with that.
But a piper with his piping ways,
Has me puzzling for days and days.
No, I would rather put up with a cat.
Now beat it.
Claude Sure, Rat.
Top Give me my title, Top Rat.
Claude Sure, Top Rat.
Top Now hoppit. I said HOPPIT!

Claude hops out up C

Now for the election.
I'll disguise myself as a people,
To make sure their selection
Is for that dumb cat,
I'll make of him a mat,
To decorate my front room.

The Duchess and Burgher enter, with Townspeople, from different directions

Mayor We, the Mayor and Corporation, are here to decide.
Which candidate will occupy the place
Of rat catcher to the town of Hamelin.

And rid the town of its disgrace,
Of a plague of rats which makes us lose face,
And makes of us the laughing stock,
Of all of Europe, from London to Vladivostock.
Bring the candidates here, to announce their names and credentials.
We shan't dilly dally with incidentals.

Aunty Hamps, Pally and Polly enter down R

Hamps Are we in time?
Polly Have you voted yet?
Pally Is it decided?
Hamps Just in time, sorry I'm late, I got my finger stuck in the marmalade.
Burgher We're just judging the candidates now.
First on the list, Claude the Cat.
Step forward and announce your scheme,
Whereby you would fulfil our dream,
And rid us of the very first and last rat.

Claude enters up C

Claude My Lord Mayor, Burghers, Duchess . . .
Citizens, common folk, ladies and gentlemen
It would give me great honour,
And I would esteem it a great privilege . . .
Hamps Get on with it.
Never mind this banality,
Show us your ability.
Pally If he has any.
Mayor Show us what you can do.
Burgher Demonstrate your techniques.
Claude O.K. Here I go, with the full repertoire of my skill.
When you see me at work you'll think I fit the bill.
First, on my list of tactics,
To show my guile—
If you'll bear with me a while . . .
Cheese! Glue! Nets! Snares!
These are my rat catching wares.

Claude demonstrates his abortive methods with the use of nets, baskets, traps and what not, but they all fail

Mayor If that's your full range of tricks to show
We'd like to see before we let you know.
The other candidate—we haven't tried.
What was his name again? The Piper Pied?
All The Pied Piper.

The Pied Piper enters down L

Act I   33

SONG 11 (reprise): Pied Piper Play Your Tune

Polly ⎱   Pied Piper, play us your tune,
Pally ⎰   Play it sweet and play it soon.
        As soft as the gentle breeze,
        Or the whisper of the trees.
        Listen to the lovely melody,
        It's played for you,
        It's played for me.

        Light as a feather on a lark's wing.
        Sweet as the plucking of a harp string.
        Soft as the breeze through the trees
        Gentle as the buzzing of the bees.
        Sweeter than you've heard before.
        Play on, Piper, play on more.

        Pied Piper, play us your tune,
        Play it sweet and play it soon.
        Listen to the lovely melody,
        It's played for you,
        It's played for me.

Hamps   Sweet as the whisper of a Latin Prince.
        Bubbly as the bubble of my hair rinse,
        Gentle as the words of a handsome beau,
        Husky as the best man that I know.
        I do believe it's turning me on,
        Play on, Piper, please play on.

Duchess   It sounds like the gold coins in my money box,
        Like the turn of the key in my treasury locks.
        Like the rustle of my silk it lingers,
        Like ill-gotten wealth through my fingers.
        This tune makes me feel more greedy.
        Play on, Piper—forever if need be . . .

Burgher   It plays like a cargo ship tying at the quay
        Chock-full of riches just for me,
        Barrels of wine and boxes of furs,
        A sound of profit when it occurs.
        This tune makes me delight,
        Play on, Piper, into the night.

Mayor   This sounds like the clink of my Mayoral chain,
        Which I want to wear again and again.
        It sounds like the banquets in the Town Hall,
        And of the music played at my ball.
        But just a minute—we're turning aside.
        Stop now, Piper—we're here to decide . . .

The music stops

Piper   I'm sorry, my good Lord Mayor,

| | And you the Corporation,
I'm just giving a demonstration
Of how my pipes can work at your behest,
To make folks dance, or rid them of pests.
| --- | --- |
| Mayor | That's all very well, but what are your credentials?
Have you made it work before? |
| Piper | It has worked before.
And here I stake my reputation.
Before you and your deputation.
Poor Piper as I am,
In Tartary I freed the Cham,
Last June, from his huge swarm of gnats.
I eased in Asia, the Mizam,
Of a monstrous brood of vampire bats.
In India I freed the Rajah,
From his swarm of flying lice,
And in Russia, on a scale much larger.
I cleared the Czar of a plague of mice.

Anything that comes in swarms, or plagues,
Or shoals, or schools, or by their million.
I can charm them in their billion.
Make up your mind, for I can't stay.
I must be soon on my way. |
Polly	Oh, you must have the Pied Piper.
Pally	Yes, choose the Piper, Mr Mayor.
Mayor	Keep quiet, we don't listen to children.
Duchess	No, we have other uses for children.
Mayor	Well, the Piper seems very impressive,
And yet the Cat has been tested and tried.
This makes me feel very pensive,
Knowing which one to decide.
Is it the Cat?
All	Or is it the Piper?
Hamps	Let's take a vote on it.
All	Yes, a vote.
Top (*whispering to the audience*)	This situation's getting desperate.
I'll disguise myself as an official, vote counter,
And swing the decision.
(*To the Mayor*)
Lord Mayor, let them have a show of hands.
I'll count the vote, I'll need two officials of note.
Countess, count all hands that vote for Cat,
I'm not a Civil Servant I'm Top Rat . . .
As for you, Cat, this is a job you can't decline,
I'll scratch your back, you scratch mine.
O.K., Lord Mayor, time to decide.

Act I

Mayor All right, everyone here has a right to vote.
And I want you all to note,
First, we'll vote for the Piper in yellow and red,
If you want him put your hand above your head.

Top Rat, Duchess and Claude count

Top Not many at all.
Duchess A poor showing, I can't see any.
Claude Poor Piper—just one or two, most are down.
Top Now, who wants Claude the Cat?
Hands up, not down,
Here, here, a dozen over here—
A gang quite enthusiastic near . . .
More—this is a tidal wave, an avalanche.
It's Claude the Cat who gets the chance.

They swing the vote. The Children are amazed and disappointed at the vote but do not respond

Top It's a thousand to Claude, the feline candidate—
Duchess And hardly any for the Piper.
Top We'll give you half a dozen, mate.
Mayor I'm sorry, Piper, but Hamelin has voted you out.
I'm afraid, this job, you are without.
Piper (*looking at Top Rat and the Duchess knowingly*)
Never mind, I'm never without work to do.
I can move on.
Polly But where will you go, Piper?
Pally Where will you find work?
Piper Not far from here,
There is a herd of fallow deer,
Who need me and my skills,
To lead them to pastures in the hills.

And further on in the sea,
A shoal of salmon rely on me,
To play them safe upstream,
To the brooklet of their dream.

And I know a flight of geese
Who each year at this time release
Their wings and homeward fly
And I direct them through the sky.
Pally Must you go, Piper?
Polly We'll miss you.
Piper Don't worry, if you ever need me,
This tune whistled night or morn,
Will travel over the countryside
Flying and singing far a wide,
And will ensure of my return.

The Pied Piper plays a tune, then goes

All   Good-bye, Piper, good-bye...
Claude   And now, down to business.
             Rats, I think you said the problem was.
All   Yes, rats.
             They fight the dogs and tease the cats,
             They rock the babies in their cradles,
             They eat the cheeses out of the vats,
             They even lick the cook's own ladle...
Claude   Consider the problem—OVER.
All   Rats, they're everywhere,
             In the corners, down the stairs.
             In the loft, making a lair,
             Up in the bower, any old hour,
             In the cupboards, like old Mother Hubbard,
             In their fashion, they've taken possession.
Claude   I'll spiflicate them.
All   Rats,
             They split open the kegs of salted sprats,
             Make nests inside men's Sunday hats,
             And even spoil the women's chats,
             By drowning their speaking,
             With shrieking and squeaking,
             In fifty different sharps and flats.
Claude   Your problems are over,
             Because I'm king of the rat catchers.
             Rats,
             No more will spoil old Hamelin town,
             I'll run them out and knock them down.
             You'll hear them sigh and see them frown.
             When I get started,
             They'll soon be departed.
             I'm the rat catcher of great renown.

All cheer, and chair Claude off, down R—

The Lights fade

ACT II

Claude enters down C with his Rat Device

Claude Hi folks, glad to see you're settled down,
Now to drive the rats from Hamelin town,
Don't leave any crisps, or crumbs,
These rats will have them off you in a trice.
Now here is my secret invention,
It's called a Rat Device...

Polly and Pally enter, Pally on his scooter

Polly It's called—
Pally What?
Claude My Rat Device.
Polly How does it work?
Claude I'll explain, step by step,
Stage by stage,
Until I've got them in my cage.
First, I summons the rats.
Pally Summon them? Will they come?
Claude Yeah, when I blow my cheesespeaker,
Or bacon announcer.
Polly Surely, they're too clever to fall for that?
Claude Rats clever? You must be joking.
I'll have them while the beans are soaking.

Claude blows his cheesespeaker

Top Rat comes along down L

He goes to the trap.

Top Rat does so

He reaches for the cheese, and when
He does so, he falls into the basket.
Top Say, is this good quality cheese?
Claude The best. Now he leans for it—and topples.
Top What sort of cheese is it? I mean brand:
Cheddar, or Cheshire, or something grand.
Gorgonzola? Stilton? Maybe Edam,
Or Wensleydale?
I'm a connoiseur of cheese and ham.
Claude It is the best.

Top   O.K. Cut me half-a-pound and wrap it up,
Send it round to my place, hurry up.

Top Rat goes

Polly   That wasn't very successful.
Pally   He didn't fall into it.
Claude   The next time is a certainty,
I'll blow the cheesespeaker.
Here he comes . . .

Pensioner Rat enters down R

Pensioner My, my, what a lovely smell to please.
I do believe it's a slice of cheese.
Claude   It is cheese, sir.
Pensioner Well, well, where is it?
Claude   Try up the steps.
Pensioner Don't know if my old bones will manage.
Still, it smells remarkably nice.
There we are, no damage . . .

Pensioner Rat walks along, surveys it, pulls it to himself with his walking-stick, and walks off up C

Thank you . . .
Polly   Well, Claude Cat?
Pally   What now? The Rat Device doesn't seem the height of success.
If you don't get results soon you'll be in an awful mess.
Claude   Don't worry, I'll modify the Device.
A stronger cheese,
The rats to tease.
A slippery plank,
Will play the prank.
A further drop.
Their tricks will stop.
I've got faith in my Rat Device.
Call the Mayor, call the folks,
We've had enough of these rats' jokes,
Today we put the rat trap into action.
We'll cut these rats down to a fraction.

Claude, Polly and Pally run off. The Rats run on

Top   O.K. Boys, pull in the bait.

They scamper up and pull in the bait hook

Now, I've been studying this stupid cat,
And his favourite dish,
I think I'm right in saying,
It's fish.
A bit of skate, or cod, he can't refuse.

Bar	Now we'll put his neck in the noose. All baited up, boys? Sure, Top Rat.
Star	Dangling at the ready.
Top	Now scarper, as for me, I'll dress up in my human dress, Like a townsman in my top hat and specs. I'll mingle with the crowd and pay respects.

The Rats go. Claude enters with the Mayor and the crowd down L. They are puffing and panting as if having run up a steep hill

Claude	Mr Mayor, this is the invention, With which it is my intention, To rid the town of the pest and vermin, And to this end I will determine, To put my plan into action, If it meets with your satisfaction.
Mayor	But will it work?
Claude	Will it work? Will it work? Ha ha! Will it work. Once the rats get wind of that bait. Coming down on the wind, They'll go mad and bring their mate, They'll lift their nostrils up and sniff, And their tails will go quite stiff.

Claude's tail stiffens, with a special device

	That's queer, I could have sworn I baited it with cheese, But that smell that comes on the breeze, Isn't Brie, and isn't Gorgonzola and isn't Cheddar. Surely I haven't made an error? That smell is fish, or I'm a clod. It's a piece of plaice, no, it could be cod.
All	IT IS COD.

Claude reaches out and falls into the trap

You see folks, it works.
You're going to be rid of the rats.

SONG 12: We're Going To Be Rid Of The Rats

All	We're going to be rid of the rats, We're going to be rid of the rats. Ring the bells till they rock the steeple, Break the news to the Hamelin people, Rush all out and get long poles, Poke out the nests and block up the holes, Leave in our town not one trace, Where a rat has shown his face.

Let's have a dance in the Market Place
We're going to be rid of the rats . . .

They go in all directions. Top Rat enters down R

Top So, they think they're going to be rid of the rats?
No way, on the contrary,
We're going to be rid of them.
We have conspired with the Duchess,
To drive out the people to another land,
And take this town ourselves in hand.
Parliament will be dismissed,
The sound of folks will not be missed,
Here comes the Duchess to start our scheme,
This isn't the time to stand and dream.

The Duchess enters down R

Duchess The play is under way,
For you to take over Hamelin, if I can stay
Powerful in my Palace to rule my way.
Top Agreed.
Duchess But first, the children.
I want them in my power now.
Top Hi, hang on, we have the very thing here.
A Rat Device,
Can be adapted to catch children,
Bring me sweets and candy and all things nice.
Two can play at this catching game.
They bait for us, we'll do the same.

The other Rats enter and load up the device with sweets. One Rat has a guitar to accompany the song

SONG 13: I Want Children

Duchess (*singing*)
I want children to be my slaves.
Think of all the money it saves,
I'll drive them daily to their work,
See to it they never shirk.
I want children to be my slaves.

I want children to be my minions,
Cleaning dishes by their millions.
Night and day I'll make them toil,
Indoors, or outside tilling soil,
I want children to be my minions.

I want children to be my prisoners,
Away from all of the parishioners,

Act II

	They'll be on their bended knees.
	I'll break their backs if they don't please.
	I want children to be my prisoners.
Top	O.K., Duchess, we're spring loaded.
	Then once the children we've abducted,
	A rat war can be conducted.
Bar	Here they come, Top Rat, all unsuspecting.
Top	Let's disappear while they're inspecting.

Polly and Pally enter with Aunty Hamps down C

The Rats freeze. One Rat becomes a bench and the others and the Duchess sit on him. They hide behind the Rat Times

Hamps	Come on, you two, shopping with me.
Pally	Oh, we're always shopping, Aunty Hamps.
Hamps	What do you think I'm always doing?
	Look at these fingers, worn to the bone.
	That's with doing my shopping all alone.
Polly	Do you really need us?
Hamps	Yes, to carry my bags, when they're full.
Pally	What are you getting?
Polly	Will it be all that heavy?
Pally	What will you want us to carry?
Hamps	I'm buying half a stone of potatoes, they're not light,
	A hundredweight of coal to light the fire tonight.
	Two pounds of carrots and some swedes,
	And three pounds of flour to fulfil my needs.
Pally	We never thought, before we ate—
Polly	You had to carry all that weight.
Pally	Well, in that case we better come.
Polly	We should have brought a wheelbarrow.
Hamps (*to the audience*)	
	I'm not really getting all these things,
	But the trouble is I'm afraid to let them out of my sight.
	There's been such grave rumours about rats' pranks,
	They're up to something all right.

To Pally and Polly

        Oh, I'll do the shopping on my own,
           and you can tarry,
        I'll get the tradesmen to send what I can't carry.
        But you must promise not to fall for any rat's tricks,
        Even then my conscience pricks.

Pally } Polly }	Promise.
Hamps	It still don't feel easy.
	These rats being naughty makes me queasy.
	Still, I must put aside my doubt.

If there's any trouble, give out a shout,
And I'll be back, in a flash—
Even if I'm in the shop counting out my cash.

Aunty Hamps goes off down R

Polly Right, what shall we play?
Pally We'll play Claude the Cat, hunting Top Rat.
You hide, and I'll chase,
Sniff you out and find you till we're face to face.
Polly I'm not sure I want to be a rat.
Pally All right, cissie, I'll be Top Rat,
You be Claude the Cat.
Polly I'm Claude the Cat, with flashing eye,
The king of all the friskers.
I'm very proud and tell the crowd,
And I wear military whiskers.
Pally I'm Top Rat, with swishing tail,
The boss of all the mob,
I'm very slick, I do my trick,
To keep Claude at his job.

They play, then sniff the air

Polly But what's that beautiful smell?
Pally Smell? Yes, I've got it now.
Polly It lingers in the nostrils.
Pally Draws you to it.
Polly Tempts you along.
Duchess ⎫ Our plan, it's working, we are full of glee.
Rats ⎭ The children are falling into the trap . . .
Top I told you, leave it to me.
All (*whispering*)
Go on children, go on.
It's a mixture of lemon drops,
And jelly tots.
Toffee bars,
Sweets and Mars,
Good things,
Nice things, scrumptious things.
All prepared with a coat of honey.
And sugar from Jamaica sunny . . .

Our plan, it's working, we are full of joy.
The children are falling into the trap.
Duchess I have my servant boy and girl . . .

Pally and Polly fall into the trap

Top Tie them up, bind them, truss them. . . .

Aunty Hamps appears down the stairs C

Act II

Hamps What's this—rats—get out of it.
Leave my children alone.

Aunty Hamps chases the Rats off

The Rats go

Duchess And *you*, Duchess.
I was passing by and saw them in danger,
I was rescuing them when you appeared.
Hamps Oh, rescuing them? Why, thank you, Duchess.
Very grateful, Duchess, thank you, Duchess.
I'm just a poor char and general dogsbody,
Only good enough to toil for anybody,
These are my most precious treasures.
Here wipe your noses, no half-measures.
Duchess Your children were very nearly kidnapped I'm sure,
I shall keep a vigilant eye open for them in future.
Hamps Oh thank you, Duchess,
I'm grateful, Duchess.
Isn't she classy?
You can't whack the aristocracy.
Any time you want your dirty linen washed and pressed.
I'll be there, smiling service, you'll be impressed.
Duchess Very good, carry on.

The Duchess goes down R

Hamps As for you two, I can't leave you for a minute,
If there's any trouble, you'll be in it.
If it hadn't been for the Duchess
I dread to think on it.
Polly But Aunty Hamps, she was with the rats . . .
Pally She seemed to be talking to them.
Hamps Talking to the rats? Nonsense.
You've been imagining things,
Haven't they? Been imagining things.
I told you so,
Now, if you please, off you go.

Aunty Hamps, Pally and Polly go up C. *Claude the Cat enters with his props basket down* L

Claude Right, I've got to make a show of catching these rats.
This is my box of tricks.
About this job I've been very pensive.
Now I'm going on the offensive.
First—my rat bat
For catching Junior Rat.
I'll challenge him at conkers,
Then hit him on the head and knock him bonkers . . .

Star Rat enters

Claude Hi kid, want a game?
Star Yea, I'd like that. (*Aside*) I'll play all innocent and meek.
But my conker is made of teak ...
Claude Like first go?
Star Sure, half a mo' ... (*He gets out his conker, and misses*)
Claude Tough luck you missed,
Now try this ...

Claude bonks Star Rat on the head, but Star Rat immediately goes on his knees

Star Now I'm on my knees, don't do anything, please ...
Claude Now to finish him off,
Then back to the Mayor to boast and scoff.
Star That's all he knows.
I'll hammer him on his soft toes.

He does so—Claude howls

Star Rat goes

Claude That won't do,
I'll try another trick or two.
I know—I'll disguise myself as a woman, with a basket.
Then when a rat comes along I'll ask it
To carry it. Then—bump!

Bar Rat enters

Oh Rat, my basket is so heavy and you look so strong,
Will you help me carry it along?
Bar Can I believe my ears?
What a sucker.
Sure, madam, I'll carry it have no fears.

Bar Rat takes basket and runs, but it is on yards of elastic

Bar Rat whips out a knife, cuts the elastic and runs off

Claude I got to do better than this.
I know, I'll catch a Pensioner Rat,
Old and lame.
All's fair in love and war,
And this rat exterminating game.

Here comes one now on the dot,
Watch this for valour, you Hamelin lot.

Pensioner Rat enters

Claude Stand on your guard, old Pensioner Rat.
Pensioner This looks very threatening, what's your intention?

Act II

Claude To get rid of you,
You've drawn your last pension.
Pensioner Well well, can't we come to terms, you and I?
Live together, tit for tat, eye for eye?
Claude No—say your prayers, I'll give you a sporting chance.
Choose your weapons, I'll make you dance.
Pensioner Weapons? Well though I'm rather old, and very unfit,
I served in the Rat Army, and now I think of it,
I was a bit of a champion I give my word,
With sabre, épée and sword—yes, I choose sword.
Claude Sword? Gulp. They're those sharp things with points on the end.
Couldn't we fight with rubber swords that bend?
Pensioner No, now I'm roused, stand on your guard.

They duel

Claude Keep your distance—half a yard . . .
Oooh, that was too near for comfort.

Pensioner Rat defeats Claude

Pensioner Never turn your back in a duelling bout,
Or you'll get pricked where you can't tell about . . .

Pensioner Rat goes

Claude That was risky, I think I'll play it safe.
I'm figuring much too large,
What I need is camouflage.
I'll disguise myself as a tree,
Then jump up when they can't see me.

He stands dressed as a tree

The Duchess enters down C

Duchess The children are coming this way,
I've followed and studied them at play.
Now, they're going to have a picnic,
They've brought a hamper with food and drink.
This is my time to capture them, I think.
I'll drug their lemonade with this potion
So they shall fall asleep, robbed of motion.
Then I shall summon my rat conspirators,
To truss them, and take them prisoners.
This is convenient coverage.
I'll hide behind the foliage,
And when the children my drugs have drunk.
I'll come out from behind this tree trunk.

Polly and Pally enter down C with a picnic basket

Polly Let's have the picnic here.

Pally	What has Aunty Hamps packed?
Polly	Some of her best plain scones.
Pally	Oh.
Polly	Thick with cream and raspberry jam.
Pally	Hurrah.
Polly	And such sensible wholemeal bread.
Pally	Oh.
Polly	No, she's packed chocolate cake instead.
Pally	Hurrah.
Polly	And a tart, I think it's rhubarb, sour and sharp.
Pally	Oh.
Polly	No, it's her sweetest custard tart.
Pally	Hurrah.
Polly	And to drink, it's water I think.
Pally	Oh.
Polly	Sorry, Aunty Hamps has come to our aid, It isn't water, it's lemonade. Do you want it poured in cups?
Pally	No, use straws.
Duchess	And I will take my chance to drug it— And catch them out of doors . . .

She slips a drug into their drink

Polly	Here, I know you're thirsty.
Pally	To Aunty Hamps. (*He drinks*)
Polly	She wants us back for four-thirty.
Pally	That's funny, it has a bitter taste.
Polly	Don't be silly, it's only lemonade.
Pally	Go on, taste it.
Polly	Bitter you say, don't waste it.
Pally	It's sharp—but nice in its way. It lingers on the tongue with a strange flavour. You want to sip it so you can savour.

Polly drinks

Polly	Yes, it's rather like walnut, or almond essence.
Pally	Whatever it is—it makes you feel pleasant. I'm getting sleepy, I think I'll lay out.
Polly	Don't be boring. Going to sleep is no fun. That's funny, although I try to fight it, A weariness in me has begun.

Pally and Polly sleep

Duchess	Now's the time to summon all rats. My plans are coming to fruition at last. These children I'll kidnap, all for my own Tie them in ropes and take them back home.

Act II

                Rats, my gang, assemble here—
                Come on out—far and near . . .

She summons the Rats with a horrible squeaky instrument

Claude   Kidnap? It's a plot. Oh, what can I do?
               I'm a witness to the affair,
               I'll have to do something,
               Show that I care.
               What *can* I do?
               I'm wrapped in this trunk.
               I could ignore it, go into a funk.
               But the poor children, what shall I do?
Voice   (*off*) Call the Pied Piper . . .
Claude   The Pied Piper. Call the Pied Piper?
               But I don't know how to do it.
               Yes, there was a tune,
               He said to sing it and he would soon,
               Return in a trice.
               But what was it. Dah dah, dah.
               No. That's "Three blind Mice".
               Does anyone know it? Give me a chord.
               I'll summon him, I give my word.

To the Audience

                Yes, that's the air the piper played.
                And taught to us before he strayed.
                Let's hum it soft, so the rats won't hear—
                For any moment they'll appear.

The humming of the Piper's tune starts

   The Rats appear and, urged on by the Duchess, start to bind up Pally and Polly

Duchess   The children, can you get them to my palace?
Top   Can we do it? Let me introduce you to
               Our Children Removing Service.

The Rats sing and dance. One Rat plays the guitar

Bar	Door to door.
All	Door to door.
Star	Any hour. Night and day.
All	Any hour. Night and day.
Top	Twenty-four hour service, no delay.
All	Twenty-four hour service, no delay.
Bar	Any shape or any size.
All	Any shape or any size.
Star	Any child, of any guise,
All	Any child, of any guise.

Top	You point them out, we catch 'em.
All	You point out, we catch 'em.
Bar	Any kid, we'll snatch 'em.
Duchess	Right, I'll leave you to it, and wait for you at my palace. Carry on.

The Duchess goes

Top	O.K., guys, we've got them bundled.
	And their aunt ain't even rumbled.

SONG 14: The Child Removing Service

The Rats sing

> When rats do a job you can bet it's done well
> When rats do a job, they never tell.
> When rats do a job it's quiet and efficient.
> Rats do a job if the money's sufficient.
>
> We are the Child Removing Service.
> We'll take them from door to door.
> And when you use the Child Removing Service.
> You won't see that child, NO MORE.

The Rats start tiptoeing off with Pally and Polly. The pipe sounds. They stiffen and go solid

The Pied Piper enters

Claude	Piper, Piper, over here,
	I'm Claude the Cat,
	Not a tree, as I appear.
Piper	Why Claude, you can come out now.
	But first, from out of their drugged sleep
	I must wake the children,
	And as for you rats—away!
	Our final confrontation will keep until another day.

The Rats are released and scarper

Polly	Oh, that was a deep sleep. Why—
	Pied Piper . . .
Pally	So you've come back at last?
Piper	Yes, you must thank Cat, our dear Claude,
	He took me at my very word,
	And when he thought you were in need,
	He did, just as I decreed.
	And summoned me with the tune I made you learn,
	If you ever wanted me to return.

They sing

Act II 49

SONG 11 (reprise): Pied Piper Play Your Tune

All Piped Piper, play your tune,
Play it sweet, play it soon,
Soft as the gentle breeze,
Or the whisper of the trees.
Listen to the lovely melody,
It's played for you.
It's played for me...

The chorus swells as Aunty Hamps, the Mayor, Burgher and Townspeople enter from all directions

Polly Aunty Hamps, everybody, the Pied Piper has returned.
Pally Claude the Cat made him appear.
Claude Shucks, folks, it was nothing.
Mayor Pied Piper, the rat plague gets worse—
Hamps Their very presence is a curse.
Burgher They get more powerful every day.
Hamps Saucier in every way.
Mayor They nibble through the horses reins,
And send them galloping over the plains.
Burgher They wreck cargo ships before they land,
And leave them stranded on the sand.
Hamps They get in the larder and eat the kippers,
And catch the crabs by their nippers.
Mayor They've been at the cask of my best brandy,
And my side of mutton that I kept handy.
Burgher They've eaten my ten pound notes,
They must have a fortune down their throats.
Hamps They've even chobbled my underwear,
My YOU-KNOW-WHATS, I haven't a pair.
Mayor Piper, I know at first you weren't selected,
But to take away the rats you are elected.
Piper But if I remember rightly that contract,
Was given to my colleague, Claude the Cat.
Claude No, no, I resign.
If you can do it, that suits me fine.
Not that I *couldn't* do it, you understand.
But I have other business at hand.
Please Piper, do your best.
Play the pipe that hangs on your vest.
Mayor Pray, Pied Piper, we made a mistake.
Now won't you play for our sake,
For the sake of our wives and sweethearts,
For the sake of our chefs making tarts.
Of sons and daughters who want to play in peace,
Of our fish friers up to the elbows in grease?
Of our tradesmen and window-cleaners,
Farmers and their corn-gleaners,

	Shepherds with their woolly flocks,
	Cattle men with their lowing stock,
	Dairymaids with milking-pail,
	Sailors about to set sail,
	Ladies making jam,
	Our butchers curing ham.
Burgher	Piper, we implore—
	This plague is making us sore.
	Ask for anything, anything more,
	And you will have a full reward,
	We, the Corporation, give our word.
Piper	Come, your entreaties have moved me.
	I'll rid you of what your mind bewilders,
	If you will give me a thousand gilders.
Mayor	A thousand. A mere thousand?
Burgher	Twenty thousand.
Hamps	Fifty thousand, you mean, Burgher.
All	Fifty thousand gilders we will pay,
	If you'll take the rats away.
Piper	No, fifty thousand is too much.
	It makes me lose the common touch.
	One thousand is all I require.
	For my every need, and desire.
	Is it a bargain struck this day
	Before I start, my pipe to play?
All	It's a bargain, done.

The Lights go down

	(*Singing*)
	Pied Piper, play for me,
	Your simple little melody,
	Soft as the gentle breeze,
	Or the whisper of the trees.
	Pied Piper, play it soon,
	Your magic little tune.
Piper	All right. Into your houses everyone.
	For I must do this job alone.
	All save for the children, for they can see.
	The secrets of my mystery.
	Away now all—and children, stand clear.
	Soon there'll be an avalanche of rats I fear.
	(*He pipes*)

Everyone exits. Polly and Pally return with sparklers—the only lighting

Polly	Into the street the Piper stepped,
	Smiling first a little smile.
Pally	As if he knew what magic slept,
	In his quiet pipe the while.

Act II

Polly	Then, like a musical adept.
	To blow the pipe his lips he wrinkled,
Pally	And green and blue his sharp eyes twinkled.
	Like a candle flame where salt is sprinkled
Polly	And ere three shrill notes the Piper uttered
	You heard, as if an army muttered,
Pally ⎫	The muttering grew to a grumbling,
Polly ⎭	And the grumbling grew to a mighty rumbling,
	And out of the houses the rats came tumbling.

The Rats enter

Rats	Listen to the note of that pipe.
	It's like the sound of scraping tripe,
	And putting apples wondrous ripe.
	Into a cider press's gripe.
	It's like the brewer's fermenting malt,
	And opening packets of crisp with salt,
	And a moving away of pickle tub boards,
	And a leaving ajar of conserve cupboards,
	Of home-made jams and bubbling chutney,
	Opening food parcels sent from Putney,
	Of the drawing of corks of train oil flasks,
	And the breaking the hoops of butter casks.
	It seems as if a voice,
	Calls out, "Oh Rats, rejoice."
	So munch on, crunch on, take your luncheon.
	Let me serve you sugar puncheon.
	The world is grown into one vast drysaltery.
Top	So come on, Rats, and follow me.
Polly	And all the rats scurried after
	The Piper, full of greedy laughter.
Rats	Come on, Rats, it's our tune. We are,
	Great rats, small rats, lean rats, brawny rats,
	Brown rats, black rats, grey rats, tawny rats,
	Grave old plodders, gay young friskers,
	Fathers, mothers, uncles, cousins.
	Cocking tails and pricking whiskers.
	Families by the tens and dozens.
	Brothers, sisters, husbands, wives,
	Follow the Piper for your lives.

During the following the Rats go, followed by all except Hamps, Pally and Polly

Pally	From street to street he piped advancing,
	And step by step they followed dancing.
Polly	Until they came to the River Weser,
	And jumped in bold as Julius Caesar.
	To the opposite bank where they were seen scrambling,

Pally **Polly**	Never more to return to Hamelin.
Polly	They've gone.
Pally	At last—it's quiet.
Polly	No more squeaking, To drown the speaking,
Pally	No more scratching, Under the hatching,
Polly	No more scuffling, No more suffering,
Pally	No more sleepless nights, No more nocturnal fights,
Polly **Pally**	No more burrowing, Or tunnelling, Or wine jars funnelling. Hamelin is free at last. Come on, everyone.
Pally	The rats have gone—
Polly	—have gone—
Pally **Polly**	—have gone!

All return from different directions, except the Rats and the Pied Piper, waving flags and streamers

Hamps People, Mr Mayor and Corporation,
　　　　 The rats have gone.
Duchess The rats have gone!
Mayor The rats have gone!
Burgher The rats have gone!

Pensioner Rat enters, wearing a lifebelt

Pensioner All except one. Hello, folks.
All Pensioner Rat, how did *you* survive?
Pensioner Why, I'm as bold as Julius Caesar,
　　　　 Do you think I'd be daunted by the River Weser?
Hamps But all the rest have gone.
Pensioner Yes, you won't see that lot again
　　　　 The Piper has piped them away, that's plain.
Hamps How did he do it?
Pensioner Hah, the secret was in the tune from his pipe.
　　　　 I was sitting having a pinch of snuff,
　　　　 And of tobacco having a puff,
　　　　 When I heard a sound of scraping tripe.
　　　　 And putting apples wondrous ripe,
　　　　 Into a cider press's gripe.

　　　　 I heard the moving of pickle tub boards,
　　　　 And the making of jam for conserve cupboards,

Act II

                And the drawing of corks in oil flasks,
                And breaking the hoops of butter casks.

                And it seemed I heard a voice
                Call out, "Oh rats, rejoice.
                Munch on, crunch on, take your nuncheon,
                Breakfast, supper, dinner, luncheon."
                And just as I called out "wait for me"
                I found the Weser rolling o'er me.
                So, townsfolk, put your town to right,
                You'll see no more within your sight.

Hamps   Won't you stay, Pensioner?
Pensioner Why no, I can't, because the Piper left a song
                In every nook and corner which says,
                "Rats don't belong, you don't belong."
                So, I will walk on by and by,
                But as they say, "Old soldiers never die".

Pensioner Rat goes off up C

Mayor	Send out the news, tell all the people,
	Ring the bells till they rock the steeple.
Burgher	Put out the buntings, hang up the flags,
	Throw out rat nests made of rags.
Mayor	Get good sticks and get long poles,
	Poke out the nests and block up the holes.
Burgher	Call out the council's water cart,
	Spray the town make a fresh start.
Mayor	Destroy every corner where the rats have been,
	Make Hamelin the nicest town you've ever seen.
Hamps	All this activity, my mind bewilders . . .

The Pied Piper enters down C

During the following, the Mayor and Corporation back upstairs C

All	Hurry.
Piper	First if you please, my thousand gilders.
Hamps	Yes, if you please, his thousand gilders.
Polly	That's funny, the Mayor looks blue.
Pally	So does the Corporation, too.
Hamps	Come, Mr Mayor and Corporation,
	His thousand gilders for the operation.
Mayor	A thousand gilders! A whole thousand?
Burgher	To pay this wandering fellow?
Mayor	With his gypsy coat of red and yellow?
	Besides, now that I come to think,
	Our business was done at the river's brink.
	We saw the rats swim and sink.
	And what's gone won't come back, I think.

Burgher	So, Piper, we're not the folks to shrink,
	From offering you something to eat and drink
	And a few coppers to put in your poke—
	But as for the gilders that we spoke...
Mayor	That was something of a joke.
	Besides, our losses have made us thrifty.
	A thousand gilders? Come, take fifty.
Hamps	You pay up Mr Mayor.
Polly	Pay the rate that's only fair.
Pally	The Piper's skill is very rare.
Mayor	We are thinking only of the civic purse.
	A thousand gilders will make us bankrupt or worse.
	For the last time, fellow, be nifty,
	Here, be grateful and pocket this fifty.
Piper	Mr Mayor, with me there is no trifling,
	I find this quibbling too stifling.
	Come, you said a thousand gilders for my purse.
	You couldn't do better, but could do worse.
	I left of your rats only one survivor.
	I'm not going to haggle like a bargain driver,
	And folks who put me in a passion,
	May find me pipe to another fashion.
	I pray you won't be filled with sorrow,
	If my pipe plays a different tune tomorrow.
Mayor	What! Do you think I'll brook,
	Being worse treated than a cook?
	Insulted by a lazy riebald,
	With idle pipe and vesture piebald?
	You threaten us, fellow? Do your worst.
	Go, blow your pipe there till you burst...

The Pied Piper goes off up C

Polly	Please, Piper, don't go in anger or in distress.
Pally	Don't blame the people for this Council's mess.
Polly	He's gone.
Pally	The town won't be the same without the Piper.
Hamps (*to the Mayor and Corporation*)	
	Now look what you've done.
	It's your turn to be sent on the run
	No more votes for the lot of you.
	We won't be happy till we're rid of you.
Mayor	Come, we rid the town of vermin.
Hamps	YOU DID! Villain.
	I'll tear off your back that coat of ermine.

Aunty Hamps chases the Mayor and Corporation off up C

Everybody follows except Pally and Polly. The Duchess enters down R

Duchess	Hah, here is my chance at last,

Act II   55

| | My cunning net to cast,
| | And lead the children to their dungeon bed.
| | But first, I'll put an idea into their head.
| | Children, is it the Piper you seek?
Polly | Yes. Do you know where he is?
Pally | If you do, please speak.
Duchess| He's gone to my palace, to be among *friends*.
| | I've rewarded him, to make amends.
| | Come, he said, we'll have a party and his Pipe he'll play,
| | To complete this momentous day.
Polly | Oh good, let's go.
Pally (*to the Audience*)
| | Can we trust her?
Polly | We *must* trust her if we wish to see the Piper again.
Duchess| Why children, if you put in me your trust,
| | I will have you like chickens trussed.

The Duchess throws a rope round Pally's and Polly's neck and heaves them off down R. *Aunty Hamps enters down* L

Hamps | Now, where are those children of mine?
| | I've looked for them high and low.
| | It's been a busy day and they got a bit excited,
| | Don't you know.
| | Still, we're rid of the rats-about that we're all delighted.
| | But somehow the town has been betrayed,
| | Now that the Piper hasn't been paid . . .

| | But where are the children?
| | I wish I had the Piper here.
| | He would soon make things very clear.
| | I'll call for him, perhaps he'll hear.
| | I'll sing his magic little song.
| | It's gone out of my head,
| | I've got all wrong . . .

There is a startling effect, and Claude the Cat appears in Pied Piper-like clothes

Claude | You called, Aunty Hamps?
Hamps | Claude. It's the Pied Piper I want.
Claude | I've been studying his methods.
| | What's the problem?
Hamps | I've lost the children.
Claude | No trouble—I'll magic them back.
Hamps | But how . . .
Claude | As I say, I've been studying his methods,
| | How he gets rid of rats and vermin,
| | And I reckon, if I can crack the secret,
| | I'll be dressed in lace and ermine.

	And the answer is, IN THE PIPE.
	Simple, fact,
	So I've got myself into the act.
Hamps	Where's your pipe?
Claude	Hah, the pipe I don't lack,
	But where the Pied Piper carries his around his neck.
	I pack mine on my back.

Claude takes a case from his back and starts to assemble the longest pipe ever seen

	Here, help me unpack . . .
Hamps	That's a long pipe.
Claude	I'm going to charge by the foot and inch.
	Now what's the problem again?
Hamps	My children.
Claude	It's a cinch, the right notes I know,
	To bring back children, here we go.

He blows a flat note

Hamps	No, that's no good, much too flat.
	I think you'll have to face up to facts.
	You'll never get into the magic act.
Claude	What a blow, all that practice wasted.
Hamps	Cheer up, Claudey, practice is never wasted.
	You'll always have your instrument,
	To play tunes to suit your own temperament.
	Go on, give yourself a tune.
	It may not bring the children back to us,
	But it might be soothing to both of us.

Claude plays, and the Piper tune emerges

Hamps	Just a minute, play that again.
Claude	I just made it up, my own refrain.
Hamps	How did it go? Play it again.
	I say, play it again.
Claude	Shucks I'm too shy.
Hamps	Get on with it.
Claude	In front of all these people?
Hamps	We want you to, don't we?
Claude	Shucks, at last I'm in demand.
Hamps	Now same as before, because you struck a chord.
	Which I thought—MY WORD.
	It is, it is the Piper's tune quite plain.
	Play it and we shall sing it, play again.

The tune rises up and she sings

        Pied Piper play for me.
        Your simple little melody,

Act II

>   Soft as the gentle breeze,
>   Or the whisper of the trees.
>   Pied Piper, play it soon,
>   Your magic, little tune.
>
>   Oh, will he come? Wherever he is.
>   Be it far or near,
>   Please let my tune reach him
>   And bring him here.

The Pied Piper enters

Piper	You called, Aunty Hamps?
Hamps	Oh, you've come back. I never thought you'd return.
Piper	I told you I would if you played my tune—
	And my word is not given lightly,
Hamps	Not like the Lord Mayor who behaved so tightly.
Piper	Now what is your trouble?
Hamps	It's the children, they've gone,
	I've lost them.
	I'm sorry to bring you back to a town that treated you badly,
	But I am worried so, and missing them sadly.
Piper	Don't worry, Aunty Hamps, I'll play them a little tune,
	And wherever they are, they'll be released soon.
Claude	Perhaps you'd like a bit of backing, Piper?
Piper	No, Claude, thanks. This one I must do alone.
	But I must warn you that its tune and tone.
	Works a magic spell on *all* children,
	Who, hearing, must follow,
	Wherever it leads them, today or tomorrow.
Hamps	Where will it lead them?

SONG 15: To A Lovely Joyous Land

Piper	To a lovely, joyous land,
	Near the town, and just at hand.
	Where waters gush and fruit trees grow.
	And flowers put forward a fairer hue.
	And everything is strange and new.
	The sparrows are brighter than peacocks here,
	And their dogs outrun our fallow deer.
	And honey bees have lost their stings,
	And horses are born with eagles' wings.
	And you can be assured.
	Happiness there can be secured.
Hamps	Oh, can I come?
Piper	Yes, if you can play a children's part.
	But there, I think you are a child at heart.
Hamps	All right, play on, let the music start.

The Pied Piper plays his pipe

Polly and Pally appear in chains, with the Duchess hanging on to them

Pally	Aunty Hamps...
Polly	She had us prisoner in her cells.
Pally	And summoned us by sound of bells.
Duchess	Why, I was only, er, teasing, having fun. Carry on!
Hamps	Get out, woman, your time has ended.
	Mine has just begun.

The Duchess goes

        Oh children, how good to have you back.
        But you're not taking any notice!
        Hah, now I see,
        The Piper's magic melody...

All   There is a rustling, that seems like a bustling,
        Of merry crowds jostling
        It's children, pitching, tumbling and hustling.
        Small feet are pattering,
        Wooden shoes clattering.
        And like fowls in a farmyard,
        When barley is scattering.
        Out come the children running.
        All the little boys and girls,
        With rosy cheeks and flazen curls,
        And sparkling eyes and teeth like pearls,
        Tripping and skipping run merrily after,
        The wonderful music with shouting and laughter.

They sing

SONG 11 (reprise): Pied Piper Play Your Tune

    Pied Piper, play your tune,
    Play it sweet and play it soon,
    Your simple little melody,
    Soft as the gentle breeze
    That sounds like birds in the trees,
    Or the whisper of the trees,
    Or like a gentle summer breeze.
    Listen to the lovely melody.
    Pied Piper, play it soon—
    Your magic little tune—
    It's played for you, it's played for me.

The Pied Piper leads off the Children and Aunty Hamps. The journey winds round the whole space of the theatre

Claude   That's funny—it didn't effect me none.
           I wonder if he has a tune for cats.

Act II

The Mayor, Duchess and Burgher enter

Mayor	The children, where have they gone?
Claude	The Pied Piper has taken them, every one.
Mayor	Taken them?
Claude	See, out of the town to where the Weser rolls its water.
All	The Weser.
Claude	Right in the way of your sons and daughters.
	It's all right, he's turned from South to West,
	And to Koppelburg Hill his steps addressed.
	And after him the children are pressed.
Mayor	Oh, great joy, we are blest,
	For he never can cross that mighty top.
Burgher	He's forced to let the piping drop
	And we shall see our children stop.
Claude	But look, as they reach the mountainside,
	A wondrous portal opens wide.
	As if a cavern was suddenly hollowed,
	The Piper advances, and the children follow.
Mayor	All have gone in, to the very last.
Burgher	And the door in the mountain has shut fast.
Mayor	What shall we do? What shall we do?
	A town without children is of sad intent.
Claude	You brought it on yourself, repent.
Burgher	All gone, all gone—none left, not one.

A Lame Boy enters

Boy	Yes. There is one left ...
Mayor	You. Why didn't you go with the Pied Piper?
Boy	Yes, I heard his tune and tried to follow,
	Over the fields and across the hollow,
	But being lame I couldn't catch up somehow,
	Otherwise I would be with them now.
All	Be with them? Where?
Boy	I'll tell you.
	By the time I reached the magic cave
	The others were in to the very last,
	And the door in the mountainside shut fast.
	But I glimpsed into that joyous land,
	Joining the town and just at hand—
	Where waters gushed and fruit trees grew,
	And flowers put forward a fairer hue
	And everything was strange and new.
	The sparrows were brighter than peacocks here,
	And their dogs outran our fallow deer.
	And honey bees had lost their stings,
	And horses were born with eagles' wings.
	And just as I became assured.

	My lame foot would in there be cured,
	The music stopped, and I stood still,
	And found myself outside the hill.
Mayor	Ah, sad Hamelin, has lost its children.
Claude	I must say you brought it on yourself.
	You got rid of the rats and kept food on the shelf.
	But because you didn't keep your word.
	Children's laughter and voices will never be heard.

The Mayor, Duchess and Burgher go up C

Boy	Where are *you* going now, Claude?
Claude	I reckon I've got to move on hereafter.
	I can't bear a town without children's laughter.
Boy	It'll be dull in our town now my playmates have left.
	I can't forget that I'm bereft
	Of all the pleasant sights that they will see,
	Which the Piper also promised me.
Claude	Did you say "promised"? Yaooh!
Boy	Yes, he promised I would go to the joyous land.
Claude	Then that's it. If the Piper promises anything,
	There is no doubt,
	He will always carry it out.
	Listen, if he left you behind it was an oversight,
	Sing his song and he'll put things right.
	He might even take me, if I play my cards right.

SONG 11 (reprise): Pied Piper Play Your Tune

They sing

Claude ⎱ Pied Piper play for me
Boy ⎰ Your simple little melody,
That sounds like birds in the trees,
Or like a gentle summer breeze.
Pied Piper play it soon,
Your magic little tune.

They stand in rapt attention. We hear the answering pipe

Claude	He's calling us—can you hear the sound?
	It's not far off, but underground.
Boy	Yes, it's the tune he played as he led them away.
Claude	If we hurry up we'll be with them today.
Boy	But I can't hurry.
Claude	In that case we'll stroll along.
	Take it easy and sing a song.
	And before the day is much riper.
	We'll be with the children and the Pied Piper.
	And as for you townsfolk take good heed.

Act II   61

>If you ask a Piper to do a deed.
>Always work from this simple premise:
>If you've promised them aught,
>Keep your promise.

They sing together

SONG 16: We're Going To A Magic Land

Boy ⎫ We're going to the magic land,
Claude ⎭ Joining the town and just at hand,
Where waters gush and fruit trees grow,
And flowers put forward a fairer show.
A happier land you'll never know.

We're going to the magic land,
Joining the town, and just at hand.
Where sparrows are brighter than peacocks here,
And their dogs outrun our fallow deer.
A happier land, and very near.

We're going to the magic land,
Joining the town and just at hand.
Where honey bees have lost their stings,
And horses are born with eagles wings.
Everything there is beautifully fair.
Just a minute, we're nearly there.

The Pied Piper appears with the Children

Piper   Why, did we leave one behind to stand,
While we went off to the promised land?
Come, children, take his hand.
We cannot leave one whom we hold so dear,
To linger on alone out here.
Claude Er, Piper—are you forgetting anybody?
Maybe, a nice furry little somebody...
Piper   Hah, Claude, you can come in if you give your word
That you will sheathe your claws,
And no more hunt or fish,
For any living creature for your dish.
Claude It's a promise—whoopee...

They all go off, singing

All   We're going to the magic land,
Joining the town and just at hand.
Where waters gush and fruit trees grow,
And flowers put forward a fairer show.
A happier land you'll never know.

We're going to the magic land,
Joining the town and just at hand,
Where daffodils are ten foot tall,
And jackdaws have a nightingale's call.
A happier land, so good-bye, all.

CURTAIN

FURNITURE AND PROPERTY LIST

The Victoria Theatre in Stoke-on-Trent is a theatre in the round. There are three entrances to the stage, which is 22 feet wide and 25 feet long, in the form of short corridors through the audience. It is also possible to use the stairways as exits and entrances as we did in this production of *The Pied Piper*.

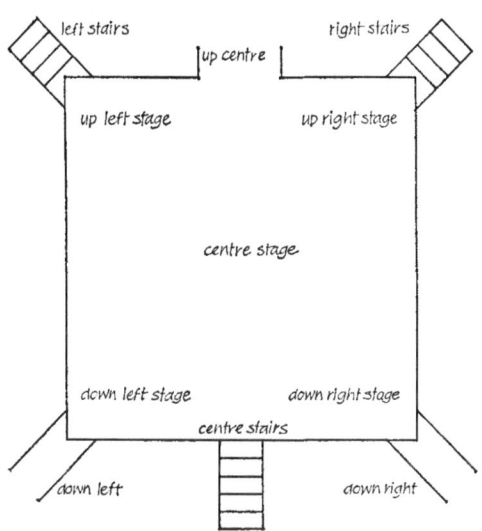

ACT I

On stage: Table, 3 chairs on top
2 red carpet runners

Off stage: Feather duster **(Aunty Hamps)**
Food, plates, etc., tablecloth **(Polly, Pally)**
Deck-chair, copy of *Rat Times* **(Pensioner Rat)**
Barrow **(Polly, Pally)**
Table laden with dishes and food **(Polly, Pally)**
Bell **(Town Crier)**
Scooter **(Pally)**
Bed **(Polly, Pally)**
Lantern **(Aunty Hamps)**
Guitar **(Pally)**
Ropes, rope ladder, trapeze **(Stage Management)**

Umbrella **(Pensioner Rat)**
Walking-stick **(Pensioner Rat)**
Gong **(Aunty Hamps)**
Nets, baskets, traps, cheese, glue **(Claude)**

Personal: **Aunty Hamps:** napkins, knives, forks, bowls, etc., if possible attached to her
Pied Piper: pipe

ACT II

Off stage: Rat device, including "cheesespeaker", trap, cheese, basket, bait hook **(Claude)**
Guitar **(Rat)**
Fish bait **(Rats)**
Sweets for bait **(Rats)**
Copy of *Rat Times* **(Rats)**
Ropes **(Rats)**
Props basket on long elastic. *In it:* rat bat, conker on string, 2 swords, tree disguise **(Claude)**
Conker on string **(Star Rat)**
Knife **(Bar Rat)**
Picnic basket. *In it:* food and drink including chocolate cake, custard tart, lemonade, straws **(Polly, Pally)**
Bottle containing drug **(Countess)**
Rat squeak instrument **(Duchess)**
Sparklers **(Polly, Pally)**
Flags, streamers **(Townspeople)**
Rope **(Duchess)**
Lifebelt **(Pensioner Rat)**
Case containing long pipe **(Claude)**
Chains **(Polly, Pally)**
Crutch **(Lame Boy)**

LIGHTING PLOT

Note: This plot indicates the basic lighting cues essential to the action. Others can be added as desired. See Director's Note, p. *v*

Property fittings required: nil
An open stage

ACT I

To open:	General overall lighting—Town Hall	
Cue 1	**Polly**, **Pally** and **Hamps** exit *Lighting change for* **Rats'** *entrance*	(Page 6)
Cue 2	Pipe is heard *Flashing lights to cover* **Piper's** *entrance*	(Page 10)
Cue 3	**Hamps**, **Polly** and **Pally** enter with laden table *Lighting change*	(Page 13)
Cue 4	**Mayor** and **Burgher** exit *Lighting change—Town Square*	(Page 18)
Cue 5	**Polly** and **Pally** enter with bed *Lighting change—Bedroom, moonlight*	(Page 23)
Cue 6	**Rats** exit *Gradual fade up to full day*	(Page 29)
Cue 7	**Claude** is "chaired off" *Fade to Black-out*	(Page 36)

ACT II

To open:	General overall lighting—Hilltop	
Cue 8	All: "It's a bargain, done." *Fade to Black-out*	(Page 50)
Cue 9	**Polly/Pally**: "Never more to return to Hamelin" *Fade up to Town Square lighting*	(Page 52)

EFFECTS PLOT

ACT I

No cues

ACT II

Cue 1   **Hamps:** "I've got it all wrong."   (Page 55)
        "*Startling effect*"

The Pied Piper

67

Music by JEFF PARTON
Lyrics by PETER TERSON

1 WE ALL LIVE IN HAMELIN

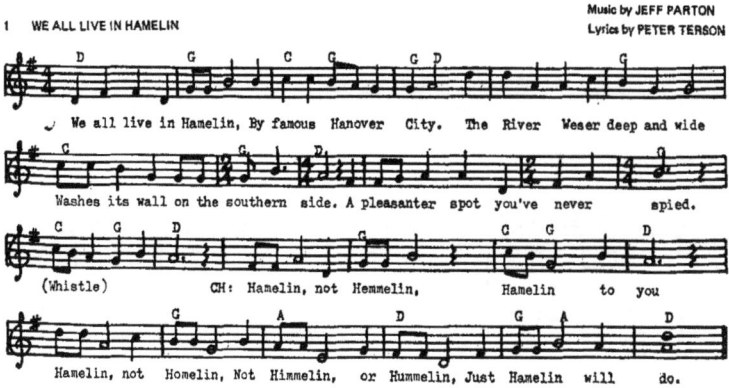

2 RATS

The Pied Piper

SPOKEN:
(MAY) In a word, it isn't a bad life. I open a few things with my wife.

(DUCH) And I rule with dignity, so long as it's good for me.

(BURG) And I deal with forms and dockets, So long as it lines my own pockets.

REPEAT 1ST. VERSE

The Pied Piper

4 EVERYBODY WANTS TO BE A RAT

5 PENSIONER RAT'S SONG

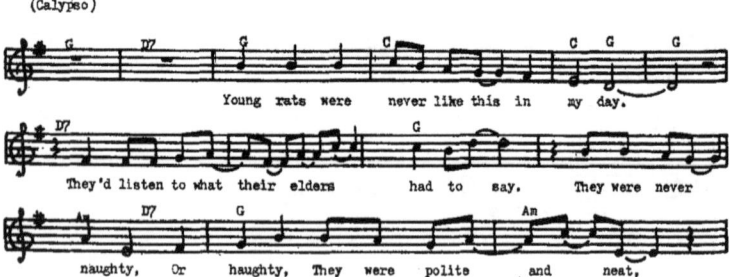

The Pied Piper

71

Cleaned their teeth and wiped their feet. They were
seen and not heard, Hung on to ev'ry word. They were
very sweet creatures, They ev-en loved their teachers
Young rats were never like this in my day.
(VERSE 2)
Young rats were never like this in my time
They believed their elders were right all the time.
They were never rude, Wouldn't dream of being
crude. They jumped when they were spoken to,
Did what they were told to do. They were seen and not heard.

8 PIED PIPER'S TUNE

(G. WHISTLE)

Freely

7 WE HAVE A PEST EXTERMINATOR

(GTR:CAPO 2)

We have a pest ex-term-in-ator. The rats will know, sooner or later, That in Hamelin we won't tolerate Rats who come and live in state, Rats who under floor-boards live, Rats who take but never give, Rats who eat right through a tin, Rats who make an awful din, Rats who squeal and rats who squeak, Rats who'll know with-in a week That their reign is over.

8 AUNTY HAMPS' LULLABY

The cloak of night has stolen over the city. The lamplighter's gone to bed. There's none so handsome, none so pretty, As on the pillow where I lay my head.

CH: Lay my head, lay my head. As on the pillow where I lay my head.

The Pied Piper

9 THE RATS ARE BUSY TONIGHT

10 WE CAN'T GET THROUGH

(Fast Country and Western Guitar)

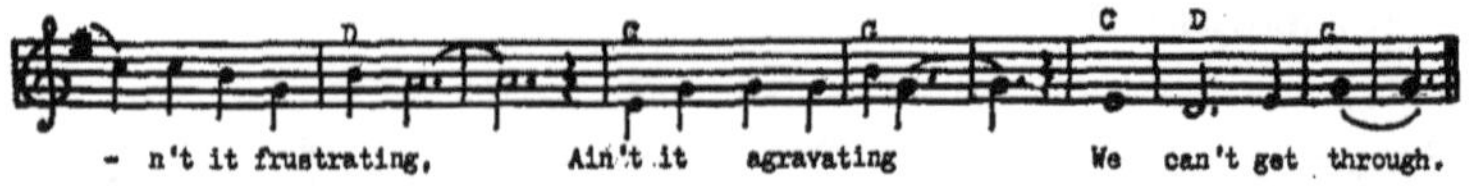
D G G C D G
- n't it frustrating, Ain't it agravating We can't get through.

11 PIED PIPER PLAY YOUR TUNE

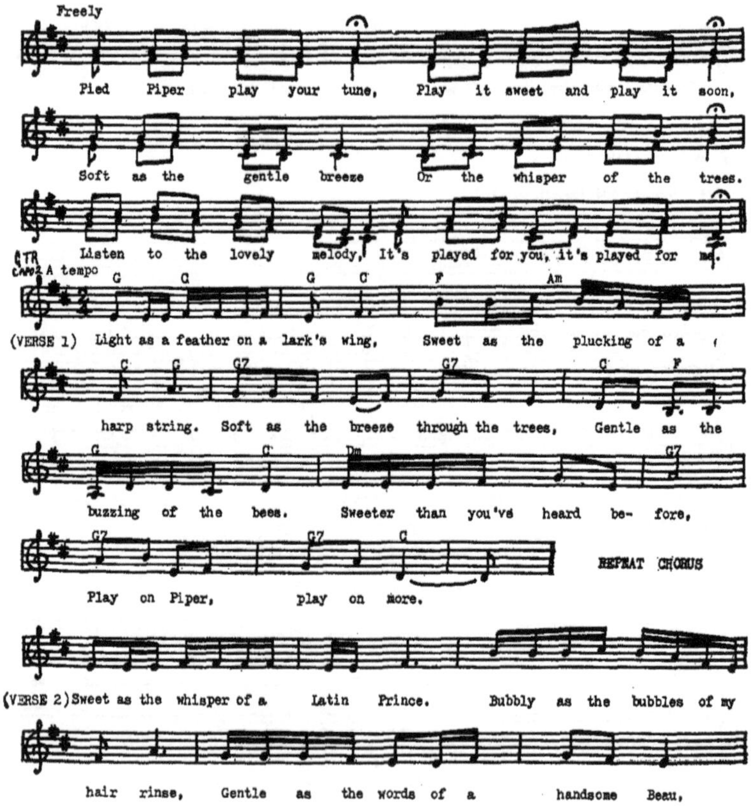
Freely
Pied Piper play your tune, Play it sweet and play it soon,
Soft as the gentle breeze Or the whisper of the trees.
Listen to the lovely melody, It's played for you, it's played for me.
A tempo
G G G C F Am
(VERSE 1) Light as a feather on a lark's wing, Sweet as the plucking of a
C G G7 G7 C F
harp string. Soft as the breeze through the trees, Gentle as the
G C Dm G7
buzzing of the bees. Sweeter than you've heard be- fore,
G7 G7 C
Play on Piper, play on more.
REPEAT CHORUS
(VERSE 2) Sweet as the whisper of a Latin Prince. Bubbly as the bubbles of my
hair rinse, Gentle as the words of a handsome Beau,

The Pied Piper

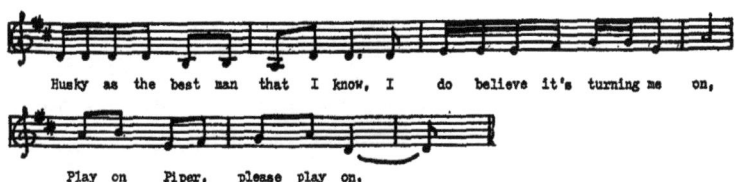

PIED PIPER PLAY YOUR TUNE

(VERSE 1: BASS LINE)

12 WE'RE GOING TO BE RID OF THE RATS

13 'I WANT CHILDREN

The Pied Piper

14 THE CHILD REMOVING SERVICE

When rats do a job you can bet it's done well, When rats do a job, they never tell, When rats do a job it's quiet and efficient. Rats do a job if the money's sufficient We are the Child Re- - mov-ing Service, We'll take them from door to door, And when you use the Child Removing Service, You won't see that child no more.

15 TO A LOVELY JOYOUS LAND

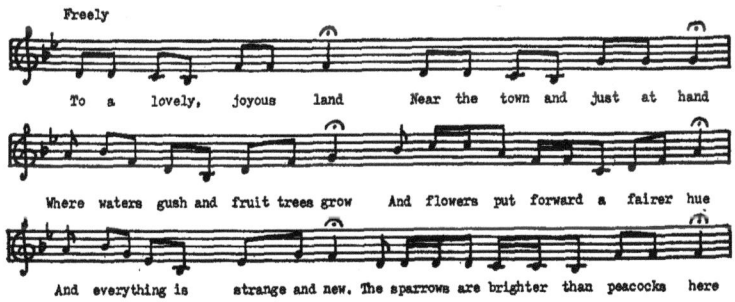

To a lovely, joyous land Near the town and just at hand Where waters gush and fruit trees grow And flowers put forward a fairer hue And everything is strange and new. The sparrows are brighter than peacocks here

The Pied Piper

And their dogs out-run our fallow deer And honey bees have lost their stings And horses are born with eagles' wings And you can be assured Happiness there can be secured.

16 WE'RE GOING TO THE MAGIC LAND

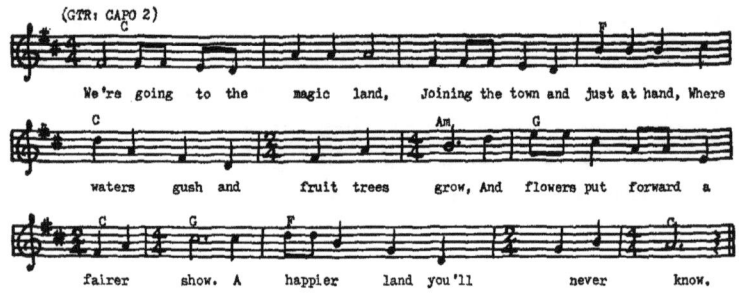

We're going to the magic land, Joining the town and just at hand, Where waters gush and fruit trees grow, And flowers put forward a fairer show. A happier land you'll never know.

MADE AND PRINTED IN GREAT BRITAIN BY
LATIMER TREND & COMPANY LTD PLYMOUTH

MADE IN ENGLAND

www.ingramcontent.com/pod-product-compliance
Ingram Content Group UK Ltd.
Pitfield, Milton Keynes, MK11 3LW, UK
UKHW021845210426
5322IPUK00022B/471